BRILLIANT
LIGHTS
& LIGHTING

...ANE
...VITT
/&A
PUBLICATIONS

Distributed by Harry N. Abrams, Inc., Publishers

First published by
V&A Publications,
2004
V&A Publications
160 Brompton Road
London SW3 1HW

Distributed in North
America by Harry N.
Abrams, Incorporated,
New York

ISBN 0-8109-6620-4
Harry N. Abrams, Inc

Library of Congress Control
Number 2003110741

Designed by
Graphic Thought Facility

Cover Photography
Angela Moore

Printed in Italy

HARRY N. ABRAMS, Inc
100 Fifth Avenue
New York, N.Y. 10011

BRILLIANT LIGHTS & LIGHTING

AUTHOR BIOGRAPHY

Jane Pavitt is the University of Brighton Senior Research Fellow in Product Design at the V&A Museum. She writes widely on contemporary and twentieth-century design and has curated several major exhibitions, including Brand.New (V&A, 2000). Her publications include Brand. New (V&A Publications, 2000) and Prague: Buildings of Europe (M.U.P., 2000). She is the curator of the V&A's first ever lighting exhibition, Brilliant (V&A, 2004), which this book accompanies.

ACKNOWLEDGEMENTS

My grateful thanks are due to all the designers, studios, manufacturers and retailers featured in this book for their generous cooperation, and for the supply of photographs and related design material. I also thank Graphic Thought Facility, especially Paul Neale, David McKendrick and Megi Zumstein, for designing the book and the series. V&A Publications, in particular Mary Butler, Clare Davis and Monica Woods, have diligently overseen the production of the book. Abigail Billinge assisted with research and Victoria Coulson with pictures. I would like to thank Linda Sandino for commenting on a draft of the text, Krystyna Mayer for editing the book and colleagues at the V&A who contributed advice and suggestions, especially Shaun Cole, Susan McCormack, Rebecca Milner, Lauren Parker, Gareth Williams and Claire Wilcox. Thanks also to the V&A Contemporary Team for their work on the accompanying exhibition. I am indebted to the University of Brighton and the V&A Research Department for continuing to support my research. Final thanks go to Tim for his encouragement, and to Milo, for distracting me.

SERIES FOREWORD

Design is an essential component of everyday life, in ways that are both apparent and imperceptible. But who are the authors of the things that surround us? What drives the thinking behind the development of new products? Designers leave their imprint on these products in a diversity of ways, through projects ranging from cutting-edge experimentation to the restyling of mass-market goods. They shape the objects with which we furnish our homes, the tools with which we communicate and the environments in which we live, work and play.

The V&A Contemporary series explores the designer's role in shaping products of all kinds – from the one-off to the mass-produced, from objects created in three dimensions to digital environments. The series celebrates modern creativity and diversity in design, highlighting key debates and practices, and confronting us with questions about the future of our designed world. Each title takes a critical and informed look at a particular field, built around interviews with designers and commentaries on selected products and projects. We hope these studies encourage us all – designers and consumers alike   to look with fresh insight at the objects and images around us.

Jane Pavitt, Series Editor

INTRODUCTION: BRILLIANT THINGS

FROM THE MUNDANE TO THE BIZARRE, THE STRICTLY FUNCTIONAL TO THE WILDLY OSTENTATIOUS, A PANOPLY OF OBJECTS HAS BEEN CREATED IN RESPONSE TO THE DESIRE FOR ARTIFICIAL ILLUMINATION.

There is light, and there are lights. From the mundane to the bizarre, the strictly functional to the wildly ostentatious, a panoply of objects has been created in response to the desire for artificial illumination. The possibilities afforded by new materials and technologies, coupled with the lyrical potential of working with light, have resulted in the production of many of the most exciting and innovative products of recent years. The designers featured in this book pose creative solutions to a demand for lighting products; they also explore the associations that light brings, and make imaginative use of the lexis of artificial illumination.

Lighting is a poetic medium in which to work. Light itself has a myriad lyrical associations, and the physical nature of light-objects gives them great potency. Lights radiate with energy; they transform places or faces when switched on, and can both banish and create shadows; they are hot (usually) but need to be touched, and they maintain their presence as objects when switched off.

The design of domestic lighting invariably includes the solving of two problems: the first is the provision of a light source, usually a conventional light bulb (or 'lamp'), which has to provide light safely and reliably. The second is the creation of a covering for the light source that will both protect and control the light, creating an atmospheric glow and directing the light to where it is needed.

There are therefore two archetypal components to domestic light, the light bulb and the lampshade, both of which come in a wealth of recognizable forms. These two elements represent the core conventional elements of design form and function, technology and style. However, with the development of new light-emitting materials and optical technology that can direct light along fibres over an almost unlimited distance, designers are no longer limited by the conventional components of lighting.

The purpose of artificial lighting may be to throw light upon other objects and surroundings, but designers are increasingly producing light-objects that are primarily concerned with illuminating their own forms. Such objects are a hybrid of furniture, sculpture and product design. They have the capacity to transform an environment, invoke a mood and animate the relationship between ourselves and the inanimate-object world.

Objects that glow or pulse with light come alive with organic properties, and suggest themselves as animal or even alien forms, like El Ultimo Grito's hanging light **DON'T RUN, WE ARE YOUR FRIENDS!** (1997). The light-object may be more than just a light source – it might be seating, clothing, or a soft furnishing or wall-hanging. Increasingly, designers are producing objects that combine several functions in a domestic setting. Designer Karim Rashid, an Egyptian-born, Canadian national who is now resident in New York, takes such a hybrid approach to design. His self-christened 'blobjects' are digitally designed, biomorphic forms for sitting on or lounging around in. As lighting they are sculptural rather than functional, providing ambient rather than directional light, and inviting physical interaction.

Light itself is a powerful shaper of space. The manipulation of natural and artificial light effects within designed spaces is a key component of architecture, and lighting design has become a much more integral component of building design than it used to be. Our surroundings are full of products that throw artificial light onto our everyday lives. Light-emitting diodes (LEDs) and liquid-crystal displays (LCDs) wink and blink at us from all manner of electronic goods – clocks, cookers, microwave ovens, televisions, VCRs and home-security and surveillance equipment. Television and computer screens cast a constant dull light into our living and work spaces. In the city, the night sky is never dark, and artificial street lighting bleeds into our homes. Light can be comforting and welcoming, but it can also be invasive and harsh. Outside our homes, we spend time in the unforgiving strip-lit surroundings of shops and offices.

'Light is one of the most difficult physical properties to pin down – it can be thought of as a ray if we are speaking of lenses; as a train of electromagnetic waves of varying length if we speak of colour; as a flow of energy particles (photons) if we are dealing with a photoelectric cell.'
Ezio Manzini. [1]

There is now a wider range of light and power sources than there has ever been, and this has tended to liberate designers in their approach to lighting. As design writer Ezio Manzini predicted, the incandescent light bulb might be replaced by 'a flexible luminous film that is little more that a millimetre thick'. [2] Despite this, incandescent bulbs (or lamps) are still one of the most common light sources, but halogen or compact fluorescent lamps may be used in their place; they can be more energy efficient and give a different quality of light.

LIGHT IS ONE OF THE MOST DIFFICULT PROPERTIES TO PIN DOWN
EZIO MANZINI

Low-voltage halogen lighting was given a new aesthetic vocabulary in the early 1980s by Ingo Maurer, in his paradigmatic and much-imitated lighting system, **YA YA HO** (1984). In Maurer's words: 'We stripped it to its bones, respecting function and aesthetics, avoiding visual noise, adding formal expression, thus becoming birds, moons, flying somethings, on wires.' [3] **YA YA HO** is an essay in light acrobatics: each individual light (stripped to its barest technical elements, then given a tiny shade or reflector) is suspended from wires that are looped, hung or stretched across a room.

Fibre optics have been developed for their vital role in modern-day communications, and are also an integral part of lighting design. The fibre, a strand of glass with a transparent cladding, can transmit light (and information) over long distances. Light is emitted from the fibre ends and through the cladding if the fibres are bent. The fibres can be used in bundles, woven or threaded through other materials. There are varying grades and types of fibre, offering different effects and degrees of manipulation.

LIGHTING SYSTEMS
Installation for 'Ingo Maurer –
Light – Reaching for the Moon',
Vitra Design Museum, 2002
Ingo Maurer, Ingo Maurer GmbH, Germany
1984
Photograph by Thomas Dix, Wyhlen

AS LONG AS I AM DREAMING
Wire, optical fibre
Kazuhiro Yamanaka,
installation for Colette, Paris
2002

Niels van Eijk's (see p.102) extraordinary **BOBBIN LACE LAMP** (2000) is knotted from a complete skein of fibres, and Sharon Marston (see p. 112) similarly employs textile techniques to incorporate fibre optics into her products. Fibre optics can also be used to dramatic theatrical effect, as in Kazuhiro Yamanaka's 2002 installation for the Parisian fashion store Colette. **AS LONG AS I AM DREAMING** is a spatial exploration of light, using fibre optics that have been sandblasted so that the light is released along the length of the fibre as well as at the ends. Yamanaka hung these looped skeins of fibre to form the outline of incandescent bulbs – the effect in darkness is of light suspended without evidence of wires or power supplies, floating in space as 'the very essence of light itself'. [4]

Finally, LEDs are a form of low-voltage lighting that is being developed for a widening range of applications. Initially used for computers, car indicators and other electronic products, at first LEDs could only provide mainly red-coloured light, but now white light and multiple-colour LEDs have been produced. LEDs are being used in the development of flat-screen televisions and computers with an ever-increasing degree of flexibility and luminescence.

Ingo Maurer has played with the aesthetic potential of these tiny light sources (which are usually hidden away inside products) by sandwiching them between glass sheets (**LED LIGHT**, 2003 and **LED BENCH**, 2002). The white LEDs emit light through both sides of the glass sheets, and are connected to the power source by tiny, barely visible metal strips. The effect is like a scattering of stardust, or a mini starry constellation.

Despite technical advancement, artificial lighting is still one of the most inefficient uses of energy in the home. Although a concern for questions of waste and the disposability of products is reflected in the work of some of the designers included here, few designers actually choose to deal directly with the issue of energy-efficient lighting. Sustainable lighting design should, put simply, aim to 'meet the qualitative needs of the visual environment with the least impact on the physical environment'. [5] This means not only addressing the efficiency of light products in the home, but also minimizing wastage of materials and resources within manufacturing and distribution. It means re-educating consumers in their use of lighting as part of a broader aim to effect cultural as well as technological change on our consumption of resources.

14–15

LED LIGHT
Moulded glass, white LEDs
Ingo Maurer
Ingo Maurer GmbH, Germany
2003
Photograph by Tom Vack, Como

LED BENCH
Imprinted, moulded glass, white LEDs
Ingo Maurer
Ingo Maurer GmbH, Germany
2002
Illuminated hat with LEDs by Janet Hansen with Ingo Maurer
Photograph by Tom Vack, Como

**FRUIT, GLASS, TWINS AND CLICK
PRODUCT CONCEPTS**
Energy-sufficient bulbs
'Lamps of Desire' project, Jacob de Baan
in collaboration with Martijn Wegman,
Marije Franssen and Angela
van Woerden, for Philips Nederland,
Sylvania-Luminance, Osram, NOVEM,
the Netherlands
2002

Jacob de Baan, a Dutch designer who has collaborated with major electrical manufacturers, thinks that the lighting industry has been slow to embrace change. In 1999 he was commissioned by a conglomeration of manufacturers (Philips Nederland, Sylvania-Luminance, Osram and NOVEM – the Netherlands Agency for Energy and the Environment) to develop new forms of energy-efficient light bulbs for the domestic market. The 'Lamps of Desire' project resulted in four prototypical experiments. These were based on the evidence that consumers are not attracted to current forms of energy-efficient bulb, which may last for years rather than months, but are regarded as visually unappealing, expensive and better suited to the workplace than the home.

De Baan developed designs for light bulbs that played down their energy-efficiency function and instead stressed the longevity, quality and desirability of a range of products with clear domestic connotations. This broadened the focus of the project to include emotional, as well as ecological, aspects of lighting. One aim was to produce a series of bulbs that were beautiful enough to be used without covers. **CLICK**, (above), for example, is a bulb in the form of a shade that does the job of both – a 'disposable' light with a lifespan of several years. Other bulbs were programmable, so that they could produce different personalized lighting effects. De Baan said of the project: 'The lighting industry is not generally responsive to change. Large companies dominate the market, which makes it hard to introduce really new and different mass-market products. The 'Lamps of Desire' project showed how some manufacturers are becoming more willing to deal with ecological issues in innovative ways.'

Concern for over-production and over-consumption has led a number of designers and manufacturers to focus on the qualitative and emotional values of design. Some designers feel that the culture of disposability could be lessened by investing in products with the potential for greater personal and cultural significance. We are, after all, less likely to throw away products we treasure.

In 1996 the Eternally Yours Foundation was established in Holland; it was an initiative that was supported by various educational institutions and programmes, and by some corporations (including Philips and GE Plastics). The aim of the Foundation is to promote product endurance through technological and psychological solutions. Strategies can include the development of anything from fabrics that 'age with dignity', to products made from recycled and upgraded components. A great emphasis is placed on the idea of building social and personal rituals around objects so that they will be less likely to be discarded. The Foundation weaves together personal, cultural and economic imperatives to create an argument for a sustainable culture, not just for sustainable products. [6] Design is therefore seen as part of the solution to over-consumption, rather than as part of its problem. Many designers today prefer to see their work in this way – as emphasizing emotional satisfaction rather than the more prosaic issues of energy efficiency and the wastage of materials.

Recycling is one initiative in design that has received considerable critical attention in recent years. Lighting is highly receptive to this issue – it is a relatively straightforward technology that can be adapted for use with all manner of materials, soft and pliable, translucent, cheap and throwaway, rich, rare or crafted, natural or synthetic. Lighting tests the properties of a material. Can it shield or diffuse light? Will it burn or melt? What shadows or effects will it cast? Lighting also presents the designer with the challenge of a visible technology. Should wires, bulbs, diffusers and transformers be concealed? Can the components of the light be turned inside out, giving aesthetic treatment to functional elements?

All these questions are being tested out by designers working now. The last few years have seen a profusion of innovative lighting products in commercial production. Lighting is also a subject for designer–makers working on the boundary of product design and craft. One-off lights, some intended as prototypes for manufacture, but others that are purely experimental, have been produced by a host of cutting-edge designers. Textile artists and designers, jewellers, fashion designers and even performance artists are working on innovative projects that incorporate lighting.

ARCO LAMP
Marble, stainless steel, incandescent bulb
Achille and Pier-Giacomo Castiglioni
Flos, Italy
1962

TIZIO LAMP
Plastic, metal, halogen bulb
Richard Sapper, Artemide, Italy
1972
V&A: Circ.505–1972

'Brilliant' sets out to identify some of the common themes employed by a wide range of today's designers. The book is divided into three sections: Archetype, Found and Fabric. Archetype considers how designers engage with the typology of lighting and the cultural associations of conventional forms. Found deals with the appropriation of found objects, elements and materials. Fabric looks at material experimentation, particularly the development of new materials and the use of unusual materials for lighting.

All of these themes demonstrate a good degree of overlap, so the book shows how designers can work across a range of issues and maintain a dialogue with many different topics. Some designers are driven by material experimentation, others by a desire to engage with critical ideas about domesticity, object use and ownership, time and memory. Some of the questions raised are pertinent only to lighting, but the majority are part of a larger debate about the nature and purpose of design in its widest sense.

The lighting industry is dominated by a number of large-scale manufacturers, some of whom concentrate heavily on the 'design-led' aspect of their work. These companies produce high-quality and therefore often costly lighting designed by a range of internationally renowned designers, including Phillipe Starck, Jasper Morrison and Ross Lovegrove. Companies such as Flos, Arteluce, Luminara and Artemide produce lighting for a cross-over market that includes domestic, retail, hotel and corporate interiors. Many of these companies also maintain production of a number of design 'classic' products, such as Achille and Pier-Giacomo Castiglioni's **ARCO** lamp (Flos, first produced in 1962) and Richard Sapper's **TIZIO** lamp (Artemide, first produced in 1972).

There is a highly specialized lighting trade that advertises itself through the usual channels of trade press and exhibitions. Trade fairs represent the range of architectural, commercial and domestic interior lighting manufacturers. They include the giant Euroluce Light Fair in Milan, which takes place every two years to coincide with the Furniture Fair, North America's LightFair International, Luminaire Asia and the German fair Lightstyle. These shows are dominated by large-scale manufacturers, but some venues, such as the Milan fair, offer independent designers the space and audience to show new work.

In some rare cases designers may be in control of their own production company, and look for manufacturers to produce their work or the work of others they choose to represent. Ingo Maurer is the key designer in this field, producing his and others' products for worldwide distribution through his Munich-based company Ingo Maurer GmbH. Michele de Lucchi has established his own workshop-based business (Produzione Privata) producing highly crafted lighting and other products on a deliberately limited basis. There are also designers who have a close working relationship with a particular producer, such as Marcel Wanders, art director of the company Moooi, which produces the work of many Dutch experimental designers.

A number of small-scale companies have, in the last few years, sought to put cutting-edge work into production on a limited scale. They take on the responsibility of developing a product with the designer, and handle retail, distribution and marketing. Two recent but now defunct enterprises are the Stockholm-based Snowcrash and the Dutch firm Hidden. In the UK, the company Innermost has enabled some young designers to prototype, exhibit and promote their work. This approach has yet to deliver large production figures and product sales, but it is helping to develop new markets, and achieves significant promotion for some designers.

Ron Arad's **IPCO** (Inverted Pinhole Camera Obscura) Sphere uses the idea of the pinhole camera to project images of a single standard incandescent light bulb. The walls of the room get 'wallpapered' with an omni-directional glowing array of views of the bulb's filament.

IPCO SPHERE
Fibre glass, polyester, incandescent bulb
Ron Arad, UK
2001

MIRROR BALL LIGHTS
Blow-moulded plastic,
incandescent bulb
Tom Dixon, UK
2003

Many of the products in this book are thus prototypical, and the designers discuss the difficulty of turning a prototype into a production piece. The transition from the designer–maker object to mass manufacture may be difficult, but some companies, like the British retailer Habitat (under the design directorship of Tom Dixon), are seeking to put experimental works by designers into mass production, as in the case of Tord Boontje's **WEDNESDAY LIGHT** (see p. 99). At the other end of the spectrum is a project initiated by the Austrian crystal company Swarovski, which commissioned a range of designers to produce a collection of crystal chandeliers in 2002. The 'Crystal Palace' collection, the idea of design writer and Swarovski's creative consultant Ilse Crawford, brought in cutting-edge designers such as Boontje, Tom Dixon, Georg Baldele and Hella Jongerius to 'reinvent the chandelier'.

The emphasis in this book is placed on the designer's approach to his or her work, from the first idea to the final product, through a discussion of the creative process, materials and manufacture. There is much more to be said elsewhere about the retailing, marketing and domestic consumption of lighting products. This is a book primarily about lamps and light-objects, rather than architectural or system lighting. This is not to ignore the range of extraordinary design work in those related fields, but is in recognition of what is a most innovative field of current design. The objects featured are chosen because they are, quite simply, bright ideas.

ON LIGHT BULBS AND LAMPSHADES

THE ADVENT OF ELECTRIC LIGHT IN THE HOME HAD THE EFFECT OF CHANGING THE RELATIONSHIP BETWEEN HOME AND INHABITANT.

In his 1933 essay 'In Praise of Shadows', the Japanese author Jun'ichirō Tanizaki wrote evocatively of the qualities of darkness and shadow in Japanese interiors: 'The elegant aristocrat of old was immersed in this suspension of ashen particles, soaked in it, but the man of today, long used to the electric light, has forgotten that such a darkness existed.' [7]

The Japanese traditional interior offered subtleties of light and shadow – light that was softened and dispersed by the effects of the 'shoji', or paper screen – which are destroyed by electric light. As Tanizaki observed, 'were it not for shadows, there would be no beauty'.[8]

WERE IT NOT FOR SHADOWS, THERE WOULD BE NO BEAUTY

JUN'ICHIRŌ TANIZAKI

The light cast by candles or gas lamps created a different ambience from that of the electric light. This may have eradicated the soot, smoke and smell of flame lighting, but it cast a harsher and less forgiving light. It made it possible to fill the interior with an even and diffused light, banishing shadows entirely. With that achieved, different kinds of artificial lights and shades were needed 'to carve a specific atmosphere out of the homogeneous raw material of light'. [9]

Before the nineteenth century, artificial lighting in the home tended to be a matter of display and luxury, rather than necessity. The quality, cost and inconvenience of artificial illumination made it of little importance to people whose working days were carefully structured around the daylight hours. Using costly artificial light sources to illuminate day-to-day activities was wasteful and impractical, and few ordinary households would indulge in such a thing. As the historian John E. Thomas has pointed out, 'lighting was not a necessity, it was a fashionable want'. [10]

Therefore it was not merely technological improvement that drove the spread of domestic artificial illumination, but also fashion and social mores. The idea of the spectacular display of candlelight developed first in France, influenced by the use of lighting effects in the theatre after dark. By the late seventeenth century, the wealthiest homes in Britain featured a profusion of lighting 'products' – candlesticks and stands, chandeliers and sconces, and mirrors to reflect and intensify the effects of candle-light, as well as snuffers, trimmers and other practical devices. The proliferation of domestic artificial lighting went hand in hand with shifts in social and domestic behaviour. With the increase of activities after dark came changes to meal times and patterns, as well as to pursuits such as card playing and letter writing, which required a localized light source.

Elaborate lighting carried connotations of excess and extravagance, although an absence or inadequacy of candle lighting could signify poverty and depravity as well. In cities and towns, dark or badly lit corners were places of danger. Wealthy travellers in the city would bring their own light sources, or group together for safety when returning home at night. In the countryside, social events might be organized to coincide with a full moon, so that revellers could find their ways home afterwards. The introduction of public lighting to cities and towns in the nineteenth century was seen as an important social improvement, although some feared that better night lighting might lead to greater social disorder, by encouraging disreputable social elements to come out at night.

In the latter half of the nineteenth century, the public imagination was captured by the dazzling displays of modern illumination (first gas, then electric) inside department stores, theatres, music halls and the spectacularly lit pavilions at the expositions and world fairs. Electric arc lights, introduced to major cities after 1850, flooded the streets with a bright white light far different from the smoky glow of gas lighting. The acceptance of domestic gas and electric lighting was a far slower process, hampered by public concerns about health and hygiene (in the form of fears for the 'invisible' dangers that such power sources might bring), and by cost implications. [11]

The incandescent electric lamp or light bulb created a metaphor for its own invention – the brightest of bright ideas, a spark of brilliance cap-tured in a glass vacuum. The first electric light bulbs were among many electrical inventions to ignite the public imagination in the nineteenth century. The development of the carbon-filament lamp in 1879 was achieved only by the coming together of several technological breakthroughs, from experiments with possible conductive materials to the ability to create an effective vacuum. For sustained success, however, the invention of the light bulb would rely upon the development of a power-distribution network and the generation of consumer demand. Thomas Alva Edison, often credited (along with Joseph Swan) with the invention of the light bulb, outranked his rivals in the success of his publicity campaigns and his determined use of patents' legislation, but in reality the light bulb was not the invention of a single person. Swiftly, it became the icon of an industry that transformed the modern world.

The carbon-filament lamp was a rather unstable product, as the bulb would blacken quickly when used. The tungsten-filament lamp, which was commercially viable by about 1910, was a more reliable successor, but was swiftly replaced by the gas-filled lamp with coiled metal filament. By this point, manufacturers such as AEG in Germany and Philips in the Netherlands were beginning to employ a startlingly modern vocabulary to advertise their products, in which the incandescent bulb is shown in naked glory – held aloft as a torch, or casting an almost spiritual light.

I CAN'T STAND A NAKED LIGHT BULB, ANY MORE I CAN A RUDE REMARK OR A VULGAR ACTION

**BLANCHE DUBOIS,
'A STREETCAR NAMED DESIRE'
(TENNESSEE WILLIAMS, 1947).**

Along with other industrial artefacts considered to be unadulterated embodiments of function and technology, the incandescent light bulb achieved the status of Modernist icon. Hans Finsler's photographic study of the electric light bulb (1928) explored the heightened aesthetic power of light and shade and the unadorned beauty of modern technology. In his foreword to the influential Machine Art exhibition at the Museum of Modern Art in 1934, Alfred H. Barr describes beauty as a by-product of function, whether natural or man-made, summed up as 'the elegance of fruit (and of incandescent bulbs)'. [12]

ELECTRIC LIGHT BULB
Werbung für Osram-Glühbirnen
(Fassungen, Kabel, Glas Korper)
Hans Finsler, Germany
 c.1930
Courtesy of Neue Sammlung,
State Museum of Applied
Arts and Design, Munich

Despite its importance as a symbol or graphic icon and its reification by artists, the naked bulb was not left to shine alone and uncovered in lighting products by early Modernist designers. Only in its strip or tube form was the bulb made visible – as in early tube lighting by Eileen Gray and Gerrit Rietveld. Tube lamps were first introduced in the 1920s, although the more familiar fluorescent strip light did not appear until the late 1930s.

Lamps produced by modern lighting manufacturers Gispen in Holland and Louis Poulson in Denmark in the 1920s and 1930s show how a reduced vocabulary of abstract forms, rendered in metal and glass, was used to conceal the bulb and direct and diffuse the light. Whether it was a ceiling or table lamp, the Modernist light was an entirely integrated product, with the structure and surface combined. With the exception of the sculptural paper shades designed by Japanese artist Isamo Noguchi, the lampshade was, in Modernist terms, an anachronism.

Seen in this light, the lampshade took its place alongside other items of anachronistic domestic politeness such as the antimacassar and the modesty panel on a writing desk. As more homes converted to electricity, the 1930s saw the growth of a new industry producing cheap but effective lampshades. Woolworths sold paper shades with wire frames, and some women would customize these to create their own shades from materials such as artificial silk. [13] As the mass market for electric lamps and lampshades grew, so also did the variety of decorative novelty products such as lights in the forms of boats and buildings, and figurines holding lamps aloft.

FLAPFLAP LAMP
Stainless steel, polypropylene, reinforced cable,
incandescent bulb
Benjamin Hopf and Constantin Wortman
(Büro Für Form). Next, Germany
2001

LOOKING AT LIGHTING AT THE BRITAIN CAN MAKE IT EXHIBITION
1946.
Council of Industrial Design approved domestic lighting. Courtesy of Design Council/Design History Research Centre, University of Brighton.

The Council of Industrial Design, an institution devoted to the promotion of restrained, regulated and rational modern design in post-war Britain, exposed the 'horrors' of such objects in a 1948 film entitled 'Deadly Lampshade' (made by International Realist Ltd). [14] An unsuccessful attempt at a public information film about design, this 'starred' a number of novelty lamps in various guises, such as gondolas and Viking ships. The plot centres around a housewife shopping for a reading lamp for her husband, who is almost persuaded to buy the Viking Kosi-Glim by an over-zealous salesman. However, good design triumphs, and the repentant designer of the Kosi-Glim gets to design sensible and functional modern lamps for the manufacturer instead. Clearly, the decorative light or lampshade did not fit a modernist philosophy of design – it was too whimsical, fashionable, feminine and homely to be regarded as 'good design'.

MISS SISSI LAMP
Plastic, incandescent bulb
Phillipe Starck, Flos, Italy
1991

Lighting, like all manner of domestic products, carries complex associations of class, taste and social status. The fringed shade on a bedside table lamp might signify comfort or homeliness; the bare bulb swinging on its cord in an empty room is a sinister image of a neglected or abandoned home. Pleated, gathered or tasselled lampshades may seem the height of good taste, or the epitome of ostentation. To shade a lamp seems only polite, as Blanche Dubois suggests in 'A Streetcar Named Desire'. A bare bulb hanging in a domestic setting is an affront to comfortable living – it must be hidden by an appropriate attire. The 'abat-jour', or bedside light, has associations of intimacy, even perhaps eroticism, as well as domesticity.

Such metaphorical explorations have provided a rich territory for designers wishing to examine the power of archetypal forms. In 1990 Phillipe Starck created the **MISS SISSI** lamp for Flos (produced, 1991), a tiny, coloured plastic 'abat-jour' that proved to be one of Starck's most commercially successful products. An archetypal lamp form, **MISS SISSI** has cartoon-like qualities that made it an antidote to the hard-edged technological language of products like Sapper's **TIZIO** light. [15]

MISS SISSI is like an object from Disney's 'Fantasia' – it captures the very essence of its object type and animates it with anthropomorphic qualities. Animation is a good analogy for the practice of design right now. Just as animators take subtle object properties and bring them to life in a succession of mischievous actions, designers suggest that the object-world is not acquiescent at all, but alive with possibility. Lamps, with all their metaphoric potential, are some of the liveliest objects around.

36–65
ARCHETYPE
WHAT IS AN
ARCHETYPE?
BOTH A PERVASIVE
IDEA AND A
TYPICAL SPECIMEN.

INFINITE
Video VHS/DVD
Arik Levy, L design Edition, France
2000

SPARKLER
Video VHS/DVD
Arik Levy, self-production, France
2000

What is an archetype? Both a pervasive idea and a typical specimen, the concept of the archetype is used to denote a paradigmatic form, exemplar or model for an object. The idea that any product has an archetypal form, or 'type-form', is classically purist, and is sometimes thought to derive from function or technology. The concept of the archetype can, however, also be applied to the kind of object a child might draw – a recurrent form that is recognizable in its most pared down rendering. Lighting, with its seemingly endless permutations of shape, scale and material, resists such rigid typological distinctions. Yet designers return to exploit or subvert the archetypes of modern lighting – the incandescent bulb, the outline of a conventional table lamp or ceiling shade.

The spark of brightness from either bulb or flame is the most basic idea of light, and has the greatest metaphorical potential. Arik Levy has explored the physical, temporal and emotional effects of light in two video projects, both of which use archetypal light images. **INFINITE** (2000) and **SPARKLER** (2000) are both artworks that have the capacity to be 'mass' products (the former was also editioned by the Swedish design group Snowcrash). **INFINITE** is an image of a light bulb that throws its light from the computer or television screen. Its brightness can be controlled by the television remote control. 'The image of a light bulb is used to bridge all that we know about light, light sources and the history of light', Levy has said. **INFINITE** is a 'light that you can take with you when going to friends for dinner, or, maybe soon, than can be downloaded or rented from the Internet'. [16]

B.L.O. LAMP
Polycarbonate, aluminium, acoustic
sensor technology, incandescent bulb
Marcel Wanders, Flos, Italy
2001

In contrast to **INFINITE**, Levy's video piece entitled **SPARKLER** explores the metaphorical power of a brief flash of light. The sparkler burns brightly and briefly; it fades from white to red to dark, but then unexpectedly reignites. This moment of pure pleasure and surprise continually repeats itself as the film runs a cycle of images. According to Levy, **SPARKLER** is about joy, hope, happiness and well-being, as it explores the emotive qualities of light, its corporeality and its sensuality.

Other designers have alluded to the temporal nature of candlelight and its physical volatility. Marcel Wanders' **B.L.O.** lamp for Flos (2001) is an electric light in the form of a candle and holder, which contains sensors so that it can be switched off by blowing. It captures the childlike pleasure of birthday candles or night-lights, and the satisfaction that the gesture of blowing out a flame can bring.

Martin Baas' **SMOKE** chandelier for Moooi (2003) – the charred remains of a wooden chandelier, lit with incandescent 'candle' bulbs – makes gothic mockery of the dangerous potential of the light source. Georg Baldele's **FLY CANDLE FLY** (1996, now produced by Ingo Maurer GmbH) is a host of candles suspended by wires, which can be used in different configurations such as spirals or circles. The effect when lit defies both logic and gravity, and the candles burn away leaving barely any residue to account for their brief presence.

The emotional and spectacular effects of candlelight have been harnessed in a more functional way by Jacob de Baan, in his '(Non) Electrical' collection – a series of lights that use modern reflector technology to turn candlelight into a light source with the power of an incandescent or halogen bulb. The reflectors employed in these metal lights either direct the light like a beam or spotlight, or they are used in hanging lights to cast an even glow across a table. De Baan uses a familiar visual typology of electrical lighting, which contrasts with the absurdly simple non-electrical source of light inside.

FLY CANDLE FLY
Wax candle, suspension wire, candles
Georg Baldele, Ingo Maurer GmbH, 1996
V&A installation
1998

SPETTRO
Anodised and polished aluminium, candles
'(Non) Electrical' collection
Jacob de Baan, self-production, the Netherlands
2002

SMOKE CHANDELIER
Salvaged materials, incandescent bulbs
Martin Baas, Moooi, the Netherlands
2003
Photograph by Erwin Olaf

The design of lighting does not need to conform to a strict typology. The iconography of much modern lighting is based on the functional components of the electric light – a light bulb, a flex, a cable or wire, a transformer and plug, brackets, screws and armature. The shade offers another vocabulary of form and decoration. Unlike furniture, which must have a close relationship with the dimensions of the human body, lighting can be of any shape or form, and it can be made from a wide variety of materials. Despite this (or perhaps because of this) the archetypal forms of lighting hold a particular fascination for some designers who both explore and subvert the common forms of bulb and shade.

The use of archetypes is a means of investing products with familiarity, and it acknowledges the important role played by memory in our relationship to objects. The Dutch designer Marcel Wanders has consistently made reference to this idea in his own exploration of archetypal forms:

I WANT TO MAKE PRODUCTS THAT ARE WELL-WORN FAVOURITES EVEN WHEN BEING FIRST INTRODUCED

MARCEL WANDERS

'I mostly work in that area because I feel the need to make products that relate to existing things, things that may seem at first to be familiar friends. This need arose from my great respect for what already exists. Producing in large editions, which is inherent to industrial design, represents the multiplication of an object's influence. I consider that to be a responsibility.' [17]

44–45

↓
SET UP SHADES
PVC/cotton laminate, metal frame, incandescent bulb
Marcel Wanders, Moooi, the Netherlands
1989

→
BULB
Crystal glass, chromium-plated metal,
top-chromated incandescent bulb
Ingo Maurer, Ingo Maurer GmbH, Germany
1967
Photograph by Tom Vack, Como

I HAVE
ALWAYS
BEEN
FASCINATED
BY THE
LIGHT BULB
BECAUSE
IT IS THE
PERFECT
MEETING
OF INDUSTRY
AND POETRY.
THE BULB
IS MY
INSPIRATION

INGO MAURER [19]

Early in his career, in 1989, Wanders produced **SET UP SHADES**, a floor-standing tower of five plain white cotton, off-the-shelf lampshades. **SET UP SHADES** was put into limited production by the company DMD of Voorburg some years later, after the product was chosen to form part of the 'Droog' collection. Since the closure of DMD, **SET UP SHADES** has been produced in three different sizes by Moooi, a manufacturing company based in Amsterdam with which Wanders is closely involved. It is the product that clearly expresses Wanders' fascination with archetypes and their role in creating a more emotive relationship between product and user: 'In **SET UP SHADES** it's not recycling the material or the ready-made aspect that interests me. What does is the reuse of the archetype, the recycling of the idea. This is because I want to make products that are well-worn favourites even when being first introduced.' [18]

↓
BLOCK LAMP
Hand-cast, sand-blasted glass, incandescent bulb
Harri Koskinen, Designhouse, Sweden
1996

→
85 LAMPS
Plastic clips, incandescent bulbs
Rody Graumans, The Product Matters
the Netherlands
1992

Archetypes may be used for their role as signifiers of human behaviour. They can also be used to disconcert, to challenge the on-looker into thinking about everyday things in a different way. The light bulb has been a constant point of reference for designers – a reminder of the basic nature of the product they are concerned with. In 1967 the German designer Ingo Maurer made a lamp that took the form of a giant light bulb. **BULB**, Maurer's signature artefact, showed how the 'pop' celebration of banality as practised by artists such as Jasper Johns and Claus Oldenburg could be carried through into product design. Maurer followed this with a succession of products on the same theme, including **NO FUSS** (1969), a small version of **BULB** in its own packaging. In 1997 Maurer produced **WO BIST DU, EDISON?** (Where Are You, Edison?), a ghostly image of a light bulb projected into a translucent shade.

Another archetypal product, Harri Koskinen's **BLOCK** lamp of 1996, is an incandescent bulb sandwiched in a hand-cast glass brick. The lamp is produced by Design House in Sweden and rapidly reached the status of desirable design icon, along with the accolade of inclusion in the MOMA design collection. Similarly, Rody Graumans' **85 LAMPS** (1992) epitomizes the sparseness, simplicity and ingenuity of radical Dutch design in the 1990s. **85 LAMPS** is a chandelier constructed entirely from off-the-shelf products – bulbs, wires and sockets. It was included in the first exhibited collection of Droog Design of 1994 – a loose collective of designers from Holland whose approach to design is characterized by an interest in matching poor and recycled materials with challenging ideas about everyday objects.

The paradigmatic light object – the incandescent bulb – is such a unique solution that there is something paradoxical about the endless search for different ways of disguising it. Most of the difficulty involved in lighting design is solved by the lamp manufacturer – the light and power source (whether incandescent, fluorescent, halogen or fibre optic) is supplied as a self-contained unit, ready for use in whatever form the designer chooses. As the London-based designer Ralph Ball points out:

> 'Unlike furniture, which has a relatively secure typology, lighting offers huge potential for experimentation once the basic function is established. Dealing with function is almost too easy, so it becomes possible to stick a light bulb into any product and call it a light. Design should be more than that – it needs a conceptual underpinning.'

↑
A LIGHTER SHADE UP/A LIGHTER SHADE DOWN
Nickel satin chrome finished steel, limestone,
tungsten halogen dichroic bulb
Ralph Ball, studioball, UK
1997

←
GOLDEN DELICIOUS
Metacrylate
Ralph Ball, UK, 1997
Produced by Ligne Roset, France
2000

The functional components of lighting provide Ball with the necessary references for meaningful design. In his **LIGHT AND SHADE** series of lights (1997), the usual relationship of parts is inverted through an examination of the relationship between container and contained. In **GOLDEN DELICIOUS** (subsequently produced by Ligne Roset), the shade, usually intended to hide the bulb within, is instead upended as a container to display a mass of bulbs. In another light from the series, the shade covering is removed altogether, leaving only a wire frame as a vestigial reminder of its presence and exposing the bulb underneath.

By limiting himself to such a basic typology, Ball produces objects that question some of the axioms of Modernist design, such as 'less is more' and 'form follows function'. He also sees his work as a commentary on the current nature of design practice and its obsession with surface, undisciplined by process, material or technology.

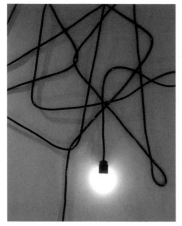

←
UMBILICAL LAMP
3ph electric cable, incandescent bulb
Arik Levy, L design Edition, France
2002

→
WHOOSH
Polycarbonate, transparent electrical cord,
energy-saving bulbs
Wiebe Boonstra, Martijn Hoogendijk,
Marc van Nederpelt (Dumoffice), the Netherlands
1997

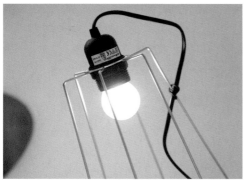

←
PHOBIA LAMP
Zinc coated metal rod
Arik Levy, L design Edition, France
2002

Arik Levy, who is based in Paris and specializes in lighting, has also explored the poetic effects of using basic components. In his most recent series of lights, **UMBILICAL** (shown by Sentou Gallery, Paris, 2002) he uses vast quantities of plastic-coated flex to create light hangings. The flex is knotted, tangled or pinned to a wall to form a complex pattern until it emerges to connect to a bare bulb. 'Electricity is a simple process,' he says, 'but these objects disrupt the eye, making the connection between source and result unclear. The eye focuses on the flex, not the bulb.' A similar visual disruption takes place with his **PHOBIA** lamps (2002), which are wire structures that look deliberately unstable, but will not fall. Again, the process is one of subtracting elements from an object, to leave a minimal structure for supporting a light.

A FROZEN MOMENT OF MOVEMENT, NEVER INTENDED TO BE FUNCTIONAL LIGHTING, BUT DESIGNED PURELY AS A LIGHT-OBJECT

MARTIJN HOOGENDIJK

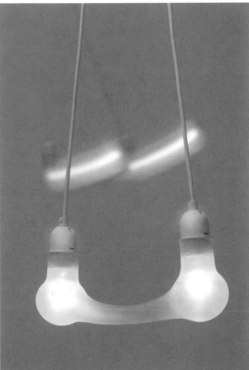

The image of a bare bulb swinging from a cord conjures up all manner of different scenarios. It implies a brief moment when something has just happened – a slammed door, a sudden breeze, a physical struggle. The **WHOOSH** lamp was developed by the Amsterdam design studio Dumoffice as an experiment based on the observation of night photography, where the movement of light leaves behind a brief neon shape. Designer Martijn Hoogendijk describes the light as 'a frozen moment of movement, never intended to be functional lighting, but designed purely as a light-object'. The **WHOOSH** lamp plays games with the eye, making use of the optical effect caused by a sudden flash of light that leaves behind a burning image on the retina, blurring everything else in view until it fades away. Originally designed in glass in 1997, it has since been developed into a polycarbonate fitting for mass production in collaboration with Hidden.

←
LOGICO TABLE LAMP
Painted metal structure, blown
glass opal, polished silk finish
Michele de Lucchi and Gerhard
Reichert, Artemide, Italy
2001

←—
MELAMPO TABLE AND FLOOR LAMP
Painted zamac base, painted
aluminium stem, satin and
polycarbonate diffuser
Adrien Gardère, Artemide, Italy
2000

Once a product-type becomes ubiquitous, it can also become invisible, occupying such a neutral space that we forget about its presence. The plain white fabric lampshade is such a product, until something about its form (or our expectation of it) is disrupted.

Adrien Gardère's **MELAMPO** table lamp for Artemide (2000) is such a neutral product, until you realize that there is a slice taken out of the shade so that it can be tipped on its armature, angled sideways to direct the light onto a surface or inverted to become an uplighter. Another such product, Michele de Lucchi and Gerhard Reichert's **LOGICO** shade (Artemide, 2001), is a milky glass form that seems to rustle like fabric in a sudden breeze, but is frozen in this movement.

Gitta Gschwendtner's series of metamorphozing lamps, produced in 2002 for the exhibition 'The Uncanny Room', are seemingly innocent objects that have taken on lives of their own. **HUGGING LAMP, DOUBLE VISION LAMP, UP-THE-WALL LAMP** and **CORNER LAMP** (all prototypes developed with Innermost) are ordinary fabric and wire shades, but take on forms that appear to be moving across the room, breaking out of their mute and static domestic places. Instead of being homely and comforting in their familiarity, these lamps are strange and sinister visitors to the domestic interior.

←
CORNER LAMP
Gitta Gschwendtner, UK
2002

↑
UP-THE-WALL LAMP
Gitta Gschwendtner, UK
2002

HUGGING LAMP
Gitta Gschwendtner , UK
2002

DOUBLE VISION LAMP
Gitta Gschwendtner, UK
2002

MULTILAMPE
Design by Miriam van der Lubbe,
the Netherlands
1997

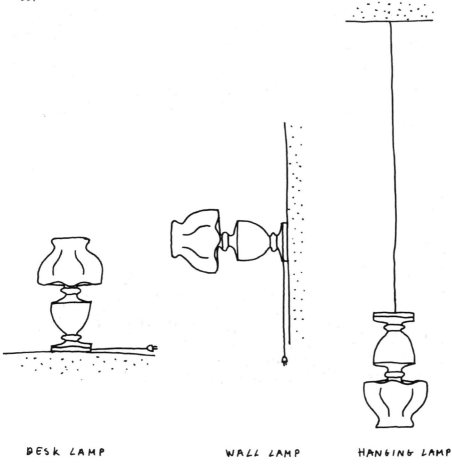

DESK LAMP   WALL LAMP   HANGING LAMP

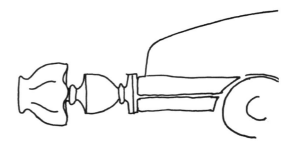

CAR LIGHT

SEGOMIL LAMP
White porcelain, incandescent bulb
Esther van Groeningen, self-production
the Netherlands
1999

In the late 1980s, the product designer Daniel Weil produced an experimental transistor radio that incorporated chintz wallpaper and a cheap patterned lampshade. The result was an ironic take on the vocabulary of the domestic, and the expectations placed on 'modern' product design to be technological rather than decorative. Some designers using archetypal lamp and shade forms enter into a similar dialogue with ideas of design and the domestic. **A LAMP IN MY SWIMMING POOL** (2003) is a product by Héctor Serrano that deliberately subverts the cosy image of a domestic table lamp. Unlike Gschwendter's lamps, which play with the form of the object to make it strange, Serrano's **SWIMMING POOL** lamp relies on context to do this. The lamp is a typical table lampshade attached to a floating plastic base. When the lamp is 'off' it must be stood upsidedown – it becomes illuminated while in the upright position, so that it can be thrown into a pool and float alight. The base is adapted from a floating lifebuoy light used in emergency situations at sea, and the rechargeable light (which uses ultra-white LEDs) will last for up to six hours. This light is produced by the Spanish manufacturer Metalarte.

Miriam van der Lubbe's **MULTILAMPE** (self-production, 1997) is a ghostly apparition of a traditional table lamp, with a bulbous body and a shade outlined in a single clear glass form. The lamp can be used in a variety of ways – standing on a table, hung upsidedown as a pendant light or as a wall light attached to a wall. Its vestigial shape evokes domesticity and cosiness, but the lamp itself has dissolved away, leaving only a trace behind. The lamp was first produced as a prototype for an Austrian design symposium concerned with glass and lighting, Glas und (mit) licht, or Glass and (with) Light.

If the **MULTILAMPE** is an exploration of form, then Dutch ceramist Esther van Groeningen's **SEGOMIL** lamp (self-production, 1999) also emphasizes the significance of pattern and texture in objects. What looks like an ornate fabric shade in fact turns out to be made from moulded Limoges porcelain (**SEGOMIL** is Limoges spelt backwards). The **SEGOMIL** lamp is part of a series of objects called 'reproducts' by van Groeningen, who takes existing objects and reuses, rebuilds or restyles them. In this case, a typical domestic lampshade is frozen, or fossilized, in porcelain.

A LAMP IN MY SWIMMING POOL
Héctor Serrano, Metalarte
Spain
2003

← —
CRYSTAL FROCK
Crystal, latex
Hella Jongerius, Swarovski
2001

←
ONE-BULB CHANDELIER
UV bonded mirrored glass
Carl Clerkin, self-production
2002

The domestic sphere is not the only arena for the exploration of archetypal lighting forms. Recently, in marked contrast to the exploration of a technological aesthetic, designers have engaged with ideas of the decorative on a grand as well as an intimate scale. The Swarovski 'Crystal Palace' collection shows how ideas of spectacle, fantasy and the imagination can be given free rein in special design commissions. The crystal chandelier has been an icon of luxury and aristocratic taste for centuries (used also in state and civic entertaining rooms). Swarovski have manufactured components for crystal chandeliers since the 1950s and in 2001, under the instigation of Ilse Crawford, commissioned a series of designers to 'reinvent' the archetype.

A high-profile publicity event for both the company and the designers, the project produced a startlingly contemporary range of crystal lights. Tord Boontje designed a shimmering flowery branch entitled **BLOSSOM** (2001), while Hella Jongerius created a crystal ball gown from mesh, rubber and cut crystal drops (**CRYSTAL FROCK**, 2001). Boontje and Jongerius free the chandelier from any conventional form, giving full rein to its fantastical possibilities. In contrast, Jurgen Bey's **LIGHT SHADE SHADE** (see p. 71) reinvents the chandelier by containing and controlling its exuberance.

Another contrast to Swarovski's opulent rethinking of the chandelier is Carl Clerkin's **ONE-BULB CHANDELIER** (2002), a self-produced prototype made in collaboration with a UV bonded glass manufacturer. This light brings together the archetypal forms of bulb, shade and chandelier into one simple, poignant object. A poor man's chandelier, **ONE-BULB** surrounds a single incandescent bulb with a shade made of UV bonded sheets of mirrored glass. The mirrored interior of the shade produces an endlessly recurring reflection, so that one bulb becomes hundreds, and the effect is of a virtual chandelier trapped inside a domestic shade.

BLOSSOM CHANDELIER
Crystal
Tord Boontje, Swarovski
2001

66–85
FOUND
THE PRACTICE
OF ASSEMBLAGE IS
A CENTRAL THEME
IN CONTEMPORARY
DESIGN.

←—
CAMPARI LIGHT
Campari soda bottles, plastic, metal, halogen bulb
Raffaele Celentano, Ingo Maurer GmbH, Germany
2002

←
THE CHEAPEST LIGHT POSSIBLE
Paper, aluminium foil, incandescent bulb
and electrical cord
Constantin Boym, Boym Design Studio, USA
1985

The practice of assemblage is a central theme in contemporary design. Throughout the 1990s and continuing today, many designers have explored different ways of using everyday objects and components, often combining their investigations with a deliberately 'poor' and 'rough-and-ready' aesthetic. Retrieved industrial materials and found and recycled objects are used in ways that are intended to provoke a critical dialogue with the throwaway nature of the material world.

Sometimes this work raises issues of ecology and recycling, but it is also an attempt to redefine ideas of aesthetic quality as a contrast to the highly finished surface qualities of most mass-manufactured goods. In 1985, Constantin Boym created **THE CHEAPEST LIGHT POSSIBLE**, a minimal light that used the packaging of the light bulb itself as the shade, and a piece of kitchen foil as a reflector. Buckets, cups, boxes and bottles are also used as shades, as are hats and shirts. Some of these objects have a surreal quality, others might make us think again about the disposable nature of our consumer culture.

Some designers also explore the associational power of banal objects in ways that momentarily disconcert the viewer. This work is often highly playful, making use of irony, but also provoking a much more childlike pleasure in the imaginative power of objects. These are objects that might return us to a state of play, where one object can stand for another in a game of 'let's pretend'. Such objects are not merely absurd (most are immensely practical, and cheap). They serve to remind us that all objects have the potential to say something, and that the banal or ubiquitous object can often be the most vocal.

POF 1 CHAIR
Bent beechwood, acrylic,
fluorescent bulb
Horgen Glarus and N2, Switzerland,
2000, manufactured by Hidden,
the Netherlands
2001
V&A: W.667–2001

The **POF 1** chair (2000), designed by the Swiss design group N2 and produced by Hidden, is a simple intervention into an existing object. **POF 1** is made from a conventional bent beechwood chair (**POF** stands for 'piece of furniture') that has been manufactured by the Swiss company Horgen-Glarus since 1916 – but the seat has been replaced by translucent acrylic and lit with a fluorescent bulb.

With rare exceptions, the use of found materials and 'objets trouvés' is confined to the experimental and small-scale practices of designer–makers, rather than to mainstream mass manufacture. Although many designers see their work as prototypical and therefore suitable for mass production, the critical context claimed by designers working in this way is generally presented through exhibitions and in the design press, and only occasionally directly to the consumer.

There is also a host of precedents that designers might use to claim their work as part of an 'artistic tradition'. Examples are 'constructions' by avantgarde artists such as Rodchenko and Tatlin in the 1910s and 1920s, and the ready-made objects of Dada and Surrealism. Also important is the Italian Anti-Design movement of the late 1960s through to the 1980s, when artists like Riccardo Dalisi experimented with found street materials to create prototypes for modern living (since 1968, Dalisi has spearheaded a project using retrieved materials to generate new street furniture in deprived areas of Naples).

AERIAL LIGHT
Metal, car components, motor
low-voltage halogen bulb
Ron Arad, UK
1981

The drive to produce experimental work of this nature may be political (dealing with questions such as poverty, the depletion of natural resources and 'over-consumption'), or it may be aesthetic – seeking an alternative visual language for contemporary design. In Britain in the 1980s, a generation of designers including Tom Dixon and Ron Arad used salvaged materials as part of a hard-edged post-industrial style. Ron Arad's **AERIAL LIGHT** (1981), for example, utilized basic car accessories to create a remote-controlled light. A standard car aerial was used to create an expanding/retracting arm for the light, and a clutch motor controlled the speed of movement.

Jurgen Bey's **LIGHT SHADE SHADE** (first produced in 1999) and **LIGHT SHADE LIGHT** (2000) are products for the reuse and re-presentation of a traditional chandelier or table lamp. A smooth tube of semi-transparent mirror film surrounds the object. When the light is switched on the object within is revealed, but when turned off its identity is concealed. The **LIGHT SHADE** objects are a subtle intervention between old and new, and in a literal sense show how design can be a process of appropriating existing forms and reconfiguring them. Bey also invites users to provide their own objects for intervention, offering the possibility of layering new meaning over objects already in use in the home.

Ready-made products are a curious marriage of industrial design with craft thinking. The visual language of the product may be industrial, yet its method of production is hands-on. This is also the user's relationship to most domestic lighting: unlike many electrical products, the inner work-ings of which are concealed and inaccessible, lighting demands that we understand its functioning – as least enough to change a light bulb once in a while. Lighting is possibly the only type of domestic electrical appliance that has spawned a tradition of DIY production: this includes lamp bases made from wine bottles, hand-sewn lampshades, and so on.

The concept of the ready-made provides an important precedent for some of today's designers. The ready-made is an object, usually industrially produced and therefore anonymous, removed from its intended physical or functional context. By surprise, by shock or by wit, the object is given a new frame of reference within which we view it, thus creating another level of signification. Ready-mades may be unadulterated, but they are often interfered with in some way. They may, for instance, be combined with another object, titled, signed or placed on a plinth to emphasize the change in their context.

Between 1913 and 1917, the artist Marcel Duchamp exhibited a number of found objects which he christened 'ready-mades': a bicycle wheel mounted on a stool (**ROUE DE BICYCLETTE**, 1913), a bottle-dryer (**PORTE-BOUTEILLES**, 1914) and a ceramic urinal, signed by a fictional artist R.Mutt (**FOUNTAIN**, 1917). Duchamp's actions contributed to the increased aestheticisation of banal objects, despite his insistence that 'the choice of a ready-made is always based on indifference and also on a total absence of good or bad taste'. [20]

This action of appropriation inspired some designers to use the technique as a counter to the practice of industrial styling. In terms of lighting, the most significant proponent of this was Achille Castiglioni. Together with his brother Pier-Giacomo, Castiglioni produced some of the most radical lighting designs of the post-war period. In 1951 they exhibited **TUBINO** at the Milan Triennale – in this case a piece of bent metal tubing was used as the basis for a fluorescent desk lamp. This was followed in 1955 by **LUMINATOR**, a standard lamp made from the barest of components, and **BULBO**, a giant 1000-watt light bulb produced for the 1957 Triennale.

In the late 1950s and early 1960s, Castiglioni produced a series of 'ready-mades', including the **MEZZADRO** stool (1957). The **TOIO** lamp (1962) has a 300-watt car-reflector bulb as a central component. The bulb is fixed to a metal stem and weighted by the transformer, which also forms part of the pedestal, and the electric wire is pinned to the stem by fishing-rod screws.

←
LIGHT SHADE SHADE
Semi-transparent mirror-film surrounding a chandelier
Jurgen Bey, Moooi, the Netherlands
1999

→
TOIO LAMP
Steel, 300-watt car reflector bulb
Achille and Pier Giacomo Castiglioni, Flos, Italy
1962
V&A: M.35–1992

Castiglioni's use of found components and materials is a celebration of anonymous design and ingenuity, as well as a desire to make us think about the purpose of everyday objects. His products were intended for mass production (and many continue to be produced today by Flos). Despite their surreal qualities, these objects are ultimately functional, like the experimental **VENTOSA** lamp of 1962. This is a spotlight that can be fixed to any appropriate surface, even the user's forehead, by a suction cup.

The idea of the 'ready-made' as a process of experimentation has been continued by the Italian architect–designer Michele de Lucchi. His work in industrial design took a new direction in the 1990s, when he established his 'Produzione Privata', a workshop-based practice that marries the traditions of artisanal production to experimental ideas in design. The work is produced in limited editions, often in series or collections that explore particular themes. It includes furniture and tableware, and lighting has been a particularly strong area of practice since the workshops were founded.

The workshops are divided by material or process (wood, glass, marble, and so on), and function as 'laboratories' for experimentation. The 'ready-made' laboratory takes inspiration from the works of both Duchamp and Castiglioni; it derives from what de Lucchi sees as vital issues for design today. He claims the work is both a search for new aesthetic quality, and an engagement with issues such as recycling and ecology. Some of the works are simply pleasing forms with amusing associations. These include the **TREFORCHETTE** lamp of 1997, which used bent forks to support a circular shade and an upturned dinner plate as a base (frequently seen in Italian cafes and restaurants). Other objects make figurative associations from unadorned lighting components. **BURATTINO** (prototype hanging lamp, 1994) and **MARIONETTE** (2001) are constructions of various bulb types that form puppet-like characters. The objects appear deliberately hand-crafted (they are evidently 'ready-made'), but de Lucchi says that they also refer directly to a process common in industrial production today – where 'new' products are created simply by the assembly of various existing components.

VENTOSA LAMP
Rubber, steel,
incandescent bulb
Achille and Pier Giacomo
Castiglioni, Flos, Italy
1962

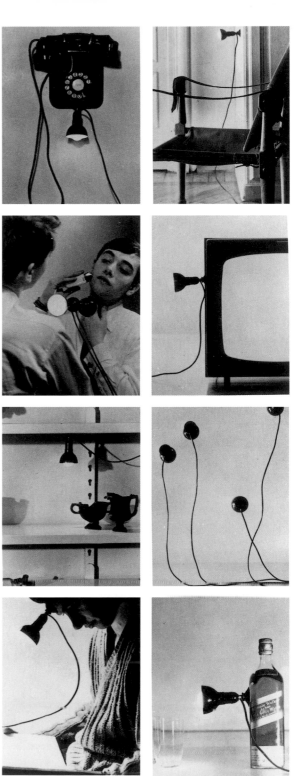

TREFORCHETTE LAMP
PVC, metal,
incandescent bulb
Michele de Lucchi,
Produzione Privata,
Italy
1997

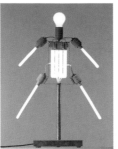

MARIONETTE LAMP
Metal, incandescent and fluorescent bulbs
Michele de Lucchi, Produzione Privata, Italy
2001

PALOMBELLA LIGHT
Silicon rubber cap, steel,
energy-saving bulb
Paolo Ulian, self-production, Italy
2000

De Lucchi's highly conceptual approach to the use of ready-mades is part of a tradition of radical design thinking that is still at the heart of Italian design. Other designers offer a simpler explanation for their use of found objects. Aside from the playfulness they inspire, the use of objects already in existence for alternative purposes can be highly practical. The **PALOMBELLA** light, designed by Paolo Ulian, is simply a rubber bathing cap stretched tightly over a wire frame that covers a bulb. 'The idea of the light started when I bought a rubber bathing cap for myself,' Ulian explains, 'I knew that silicon rubber is very resistant to hot temperatures (to about 150 degrees Celsius). The cap is very cheap and it comes in many different colours, so I thought why not use an existing product instead of creating a new object with expensive moulds and processes?'

Claire Norcross' **EIGHT-FIFTY LIGHT** (2002) is a pendant lamp created for Habitat. It is made from plastic tags that are commonly used in industrial packaging. The tags form a spiky sphere, which quivers slightly in the heat given off by the lamp inside. Norcross, a textile artist, first used this as a method of making lights by hand, before Habitat adopted the lamp for mass manufacture. The light is an unusual example of a mass-produced product that has been made from found materials. Despite the cheapness and ready availability of such resources, their use in product design tends to be confined to one-off or small-batch production, perhaps because commercial manufacturers are cautious as to their consumer appeal.

British designer Neil Austin used disposable plastic drinking cups for his **CUP LIGHT** (1998), a one-off prototype that is, nevertheless, mass manufacturable. The **CUP LIGHT** was first exhibited as part of the **MO-BILLY** collection (2000) – the products of a UK-based design initiative called Big William, which helps students to bridge the gap between education and employment, enabling them to develop and exhibit prototypical products and to approach manufacturers. As a founder of Big William and a lecturer as well as a designer, Austin's approach to teaching is to encourage students to look at the world of everyday things with an eye to appropriation and playful reuse.

Other British designers who exemplify this approach are Carl Clerkin and Michael Marriott. Trained at the Royal College of Art in London, Marriott has become renowned for his low-tech approach to designing products, which includes using cheap and reclaimed materials (pegboard and MDF), basic hardware (wingnuts, pegs) and off-the-shelf products (plastic buckets). His work is always imaginative, as well as deeply practical and elegantly economical, although his inverted bucket light (see cover illustration) has never been intended for production but is used in exhibitions and displays. His **POST CARD LIGHT** (1994), on the other hand, is in batch production – this is a tiny table lamp to which the owner can attach a favourite postcard as a shade for the light.

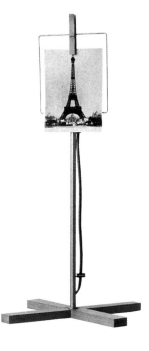

Carl Clerkin's **CORKSCREW LAMP** (1997) plays on the idea of the classic domestic DIY lamp: the wine bottle with a shade on top. In Clerkin's version, the corkscrew is left in the (empty) bottle to provide an armature for the shade, and the wire is held to the side of the bottle with a plastic strap. All the elements of the light are found, and minimal 'interference' has taken place to create the object. It is a complex but understated engagement with the idea of the ready-made.

When used with light, poor materials can perform in ways that divorce them from their original contexts. As with any kind of material experimentation, uses for waste products tend to develop from an open-ended research process, where the designer may be led by a desire to work in a certain way, but without a defined end product in mind.

POST CARD LIGHT
Beech, mild steel tube and wire, beech clothes peg,
Michael Marriott, self-production
1994

EIGHT-FIFTY LIGHT
Metal with black and white
plastic arms, incandescent bulb
Claire Norcross, Habitat, UK
2002

CUP LIGHT
Polystyrene cups, rivets, tungsten bulb
Neil Austin, self-production, UK
1998

NEED LIGHT
Non-starched honeycomb recycled
cardboard with colour filter,
incandescent bulb
Arik Levy, L design Edition, France
1996
Photograph by F. Kleinefenn

CORKSCREW LAMP
Brass corkscrew, bottle
Carl Clerkin, self-production
1997

Arik Levy refers to the common industrial materials he uses as 'blind materials'. These materials are all around us, but we barely know they are there. They may be substances that provide filling, structure or cladding for anything from aircraft wings to packaging. Levy's **NEED** light (1996) – an example of which is in the MOMA collection – is made from a kind of cardboard honeycomb commonly used in partition walls. This material is no longer produced, so the light has also gone out of production. Levy has, however, developed a similar idea with other materials.

Another range of lights (**XM3** lights, 1996) uses aluminium foil in a honeycomb form, a material that is manufactured as structural filling for aircraft wings. Levy uses the honeycomb material in its flexible, non-extended form – a state it is in midway through production. As he says, something that is made to be linear and structural becomes circular and elastic, demonstrating entirely different properties from its intended purpose. 'I consider my work to be scientific,' Levy explains, 'I analyze the materials to find their genetic code, then change them with my own genetic intervention.'

Héctor Serrano's approach to design and materials exemplifies this open-ended approach, where the material, rather than the end product, is what drives the idea. While a student at the Royal College of Art in London, Serrano produced the **SUPER PATATA** light (1999), now under development for large-scale manufacture.

Serrano explains: 'The idea for the lamp came from a child's toy – a balloon filled with flour, tied with a shoelace and decorated with a face – the kind of cheap toy bought from market stalls. I bought one of these toys in 1999, whilst in Paris on holiday. I had been collecting objects in order to find the starting point for a new project. I wanted to take the most interesting part of the toy – its playfulness and tactility – and put it into a functional object. I didn't mean to do a lamp, but I made some sketches and the light was one of the first.'

THE IDEA FOR THE LAMP CAME FROM A CHILD'S TOY

HÉCTOR SERRANO

The **SUPER PATATA** is a deliberately low-tech object. Serrano experimented with various fillings – flour, glass beads and then salt, which has a translucency that diffuses light. The casing is a large-size latex party balloon.

'I wanted to let the user control the intensity of the light just by touching it. As you squeeze the light, the bulb moves around in the salt, and gets brighter as it gets closer to the surface. That's what the product allows you to do – play with light.'

The playful experimentation with cheap, low-tech materials is a trademark of Serrano's work. **TOP SECRET**, first produced in 2000, is another of his 'accidental' lighting projects. A student project involving designing products that would improve the quality of life on the streets for the homeless led him to consider using shredded paper as a stuffing for bedding made of rubbish bags. Serrano shredded different papers, cards and plastic film in a standard office shredder. The translucent effects of shredded films (acetate and then polyester) gave him the idea for a form of lighting. The shredded material is gathered up in a nylon net and hung around a compact fluorescent light fitting. He says of the light, 'I like the fact that it looks like a luxury material when it is lit, but in fact it is garbage.' It is the idea, not the technology, that guides Serrano's work.

SUPER PATATA LIGHT
Latex, salt, compact fluorescent bulb
Héctor Serrano, self-production, UK
1999

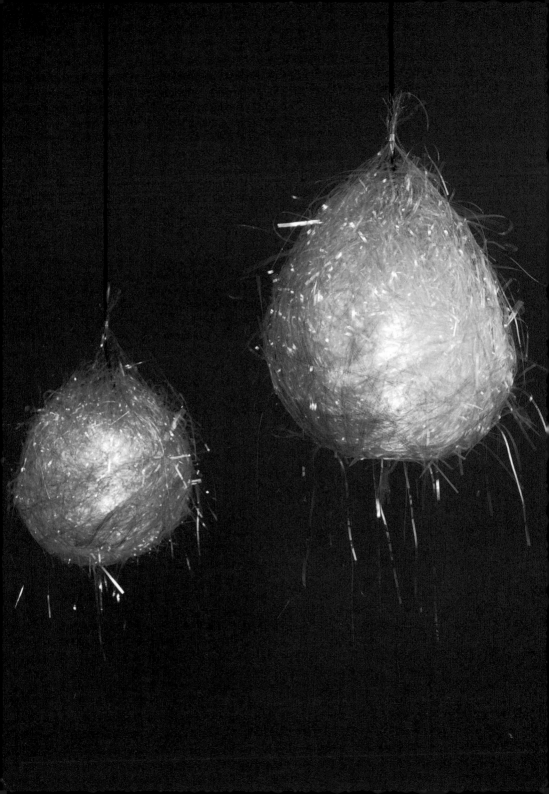

←
PLAYBOY LIGHT
Acrylic, compact fluorescent bulb
Héctor Serrano, self-production, UK
2003

←—
TOP SECRET LIGHT
Polyester film, nylon net, compact
fluorescent bulb
Héctor Serrano, self-production, UK
2000

'I'm not interested in lighting particularly, but in designing products that create reactions. Yet light is a magical thing to incorporate into an object. To do a lamp is easy – at least 50 per cent of the work has been done already, so all you need is to buy the cable, the fitting and the bulb.'

'Doing a lamp' yourself is the basis for the **PLAYBOY** light, a clear acrylic coat hanger with a light fitting, onto which you can hang your own clothes as a shade. Although the light is typically low tech, it is partly influenced by some work Serrano did for the design consultancy IDEO in 2001, on an investigation into intelligent fabrics. By day he worked with IDEO, testing fabrics that could take the incorporation of 'smart' technology and be used as clothing. At home, a broken light fitting that he had 'repaired' by using a piece of clothing as a shade gave him the idea for **PLAYBOY**.

Objects like these display the serendipitous element of the design process. When designers allow the associational power of objects to take hold, they can create things that go beyond function to engage our imaginations. The use of found objects and materials is an important part of that process in a technical, aesthetic way, as well as in a psychological way.

86–123

FABRIC

WHATEVER THE FORM OF LIGHTING, THE TRANSLUCENT EFFECTS OF HARD MATERIALS, SOFT FABRICS AND YARNS CAN BE HARNESSED TO GIVE LIGHTING QUALITY AND CHARACTER.

FIL DE FER LAMP
Pre-moulded aluminium, halogen bulb
Enzo Catellani, Catellani & Smith, Italy
2001

The search for new effects and forms is a very hands-on process, demanding experimentation with an often unlikely range of materials and substances. It can also involve new ways of using traditional light-diffusing or refracting materials such as paper and glass. Materials experimentation has always played a part in the design of lighting, as the eighteenth-century physicist Benjamin Count Rumford observed:

> 'The only way in which the flames of lamps and candles can be masked, without occasioning a great loss of light, is to cover them with screens composed of such substances as disperse the light without destroying it. Ground glass, thin white silk stuffs, such as gauze and crepe, fine white paper, horn, and various other substances, may be used for that purpose ...'[21]

Some designers have developed their own materials for use in combination with light, while others have appropriated existing methods of fabrication to create new product forms. Materials experimentation often leads to an idea for a lamp, usually because the visual effect of a particular material or form can be enhanced by adding light to it. In this way, some of the lamps featured here are an unexpected by-product of a different investigation. Some of the designers also work outside the boundaries of conventional product design, choosing to engage with fashion, body adornment and even performance.

**GE OFF SPHERE
CEILING LIGHT**

SLS polyamide, stainless
steel cable and pulley
system, low-voltage
halogen bulbs,
Ron Arad, Geoff Crowther,
Yuko Tango, Elliot Howes,
distributed by
Gallery Mourmans, UK
2000

SKINNED PRISMEX TABLE
Prismex®, leather
Nick Gant and Tanya Dean,
self-production, UK
2002

The materials incorporated into contemporary lighting also span the range from low-tech to high-tech. There are lighting uses for waste materials from ground glass to shredded plastic film, and for industrial materials usually employed for other purposes. Some companies and designers are developing creative ways of using new technologies – fibre optics being the most prominent. Traditional methods of textile production, such as knitting, weaving and crochet, are used to fashion light products from conductive and light-providing materials. These methods produce some startling sculptural works, but they are often employed for highly functional reasons too.

The distinctions between hand-made and machine-made, and between two-dimensional and three-dimensional approaches to design, are blurred further by the impact of digital processes. In 2000, Ron Arad exhibited a collection of products, including the **GE OFF SPHERE** ceiling light, which had been produced by rapid prototyping. This is the collective term for a range of processes used to manufacture perfect 3D replicas of digitally created products or components. [22] The process is a sophisticated form of model making, but Arad adopted it as the means to make finished products.

Rather than being carved, turned, moulded, bent, vacuum formed or welded (or made by any other conventional means of manipulating material), the product is 'grown' in a tank. The raw material is a liquid or powder polymer, which is hardened using computer-controlled lasers, following information created on a 3D computer-aided design program. The result is a three-dimensional 'print-out' of an object. Arad used the process to create a series of forms (exhibited as the 'Not Made by Hand, Not Made in China' collection), which were then adapted to serve functional purposes as vases or lamps.

GLO-NUTS
Perspex Frost™
Nick Gant and Tanya Dean,
self-production, UK
2002

Collaboration between designers and the manufacturers of synthetic and composite materials has produced some interesting results in the field of lighting. Materials developed for other purposes have often found a secondary use as lighting. The British partnership of Tanya Dean and Nick Gant, known as Bobo Design, has worked with ICI, who manufacture the branded acrylic Prismex®. This is an acrylic sheet, screen-printed with tiny dots that reflect light from within the material, so that it looks like a glowing panel of light. Its most common application is for edge-lit signage and advertising. Gant and Dean have used the material for a variety of alternative design applications, including their **PRISMEX TABLE** (1999), a glowing sheet of light held in a spare metal frame (a more recent version, from 2002, wraps the table in a hand-stitched leather cover which rolls back to reveal the lit surface). Their product **GLO NUTS** (2002) is a multi-functional, moulded perspex form that can be used for interior and exterior lighting, storage purposes and seating.

Lighted furniture, as opposed to lighting, is another way for designers to explore the relationship between light and space. Kazuhiro Yamanaka, a Japanese designer now based in London, has created a number of prototypical works that explore the effect of light-objects in spaces. 'I create spaces, not objects,' says Yamanaka. 'Designers should contemplate the void that surrounds objects, the space between objects, and the relationship between those objects. I believe furniture – chairs, tables, lights – could be like a constellation of stars, and we could make lines to connect them three-dimensionally and thereby construct a specific story.'

WHAT A LITTLE MOONLIGHT CAN DO
Alucobond, halogen bulb
Kazuhiro Yamanaka, Boffi, Italy
1998

Yamanaka's light entitled **WHAT A LITTLE MOONLIGHT CAN DO** (1998) was the first in a series of objects that explored the relationship between form, light and space. It is a large panel of Alucobond – a layer of plastic between two aluminium sheets. A halogen bulb is mounted off-set into the panel, and the electricity is conducted through the metal without the need for any wires. The light is diffused through the sheet so that the whole panel glows. Yamanaka has since produced an illuminated chair and lamp (2003) made of translucent polypropylene. **WHAT A LITTLE MOONLIGHT CAN DO** is manufactured by Boffi in Italy.

Corian®, a non-porous solid surface material made from minerals and acrylic polymers and manufactured by Dupont, is commonly thought of as a hard-wearing surface that is used for kitchen counter-tops. It can be cut and shaped like wood and stone, or moulded and thermoformed. Despite its solidity, it also has a certain translucency – a characteristic explored by several designers working with Dupont. Ross Lovegrove, James Irvine and Marc Newson each created a light installation using the material during the Milan Furniture Fair in 2003. Newson's installation of thermoformed **DIODE** lights – a forest of giant glowing lollipops – showed a potential product application of the material. Lovegrove's installation **THE LAND OF LU** explored Corian's stone-like quality and its opacity.

CROCHET LAMP
Silver-plated and copper electrical
wire, halogen bulb
Michael Sans, self-production, Germany
2002

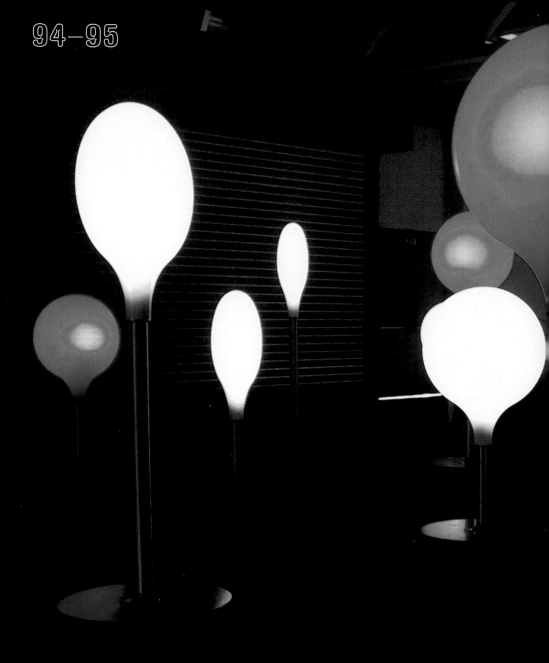

DIODE LIGHTS
Marc Newson for Corian®,
fabricated by Pfeiffer & Sohne
GmbH, Germany
2003

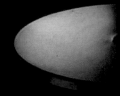

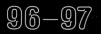

THE LAND OF LU
Light installations with Corian
Ross Lovegrove for Corian®,
fabricated by Hasenkopf, lighting by Luceplan, Germany
2003

OCTOPUS LAMP
3D textile, painted metal
Arik Levy, Ligne Roset, France
2002

Arik Levy sees his work as being led by materials experimentation. A recent light designed for Ligne Roset, the **OCTOPUS** lamp (2002), uses a three-dimensional textile: this is woven in 2D, impregnated with resin, compressed and then heated to create a three-dimensional surface. Levy says, 'I spend about 15 per cent of my time in the search for interesting new materials, and often find them in strange domains – military fairs, scientific conferences, discussions about micro and bio mechanics.' His research is often undertaken without a specific commercial objective or product outcome in mind – his creations tend to be a by-product of his thinking process. One current research project is an investigation into the luminescent capacities of deep-water seaweed and their possibilities for lighting.

The use of materials in contemporary lighting straddles the boundaries of craft and design – there is a high degree of hand-making and hands-on work in the development of many of the products shown here. Some designers take this hands-on approach even further to involve the end-user. Michael Sans, a Berlin-based industrial designer, produced the **CROCHET LAMP** (**LAMPEGEHAKELT**) while studying at the RCA in 2002. Silver-plated or copper wire, which supplies electricity to the light, is crocheted into the form of the shade, so that the light is made from a single length of wire. Sans has considered selling the product as a 'do-it-yourself' kit complete with instructions, a length of wire and a crochet hook.

I SPEND ABOUT 15 PER CENT OF MY TIME IN THE SEARCH FOR INTEREST-ING NEW MATERIALS, AND OFTEN FIND THEM IN STRANGE DOMAINS

ARIK LEVY

←
WEDNESDAY LIGHT
Laser-cut stainless steel, photographically
etched, incandescent bulb
Tord Boontje, self-production, UK
2002

—→
GARLAND
Design for laser-cut brass sheet
Tord Boontje for Habitat, UK
2003

Working with basic resources is a trademark of Tord Boontje, a designer from Holland who is now based in London. Boontje works across the spectrum of design practice, from the employment of craft methods to the use of hi-tech processes such as digital design. His **WEDNESDAY LIGHT**, part of the 'Wednesday' collection begun in 2002, is a simple flower garland of stainless steel, wound around a bare bulb (by the user) and secured with a clip.

When illuminated, the garland casts a delicate filigree shadow, filling the surrounding walls with pattern. It is made by photographically etching the steel, which cuts a pattern from the sheet (a method used for manufacturing accurate electronic components). The flower pattern is designed by Boontje and has been used by him in a number of ways, on furniture and textiles, and as a computer-generated artwork. He is interested in the potential of decoration, particularly in the context of domesticity. The collection, he says, is 'homely and loving, sparse yet pretty', and produced 'without a lot of resources, but with a lot of time, care and love'.

Boontje describes his working method as 'thinking through making', and sees materials experimentation as one of the most creative conduits for design. The **WEDNESDAY LIGHT** has been adapted for mass manufacture by Habitat (as a product named **GARLAND**), in nickel-plated brass instead of stainless steel, and with a simplified pattern to reduce production costs. Boontje is excited by the translation of his process from batch to mass production, as it exemplifies his interest in the translation of ideas into everyday products.

The return to pattern and decoration demonstrated by many contemporary designers has also led to the use and adaptation of traditional craft techniques and materials for lighting products. The vocabulary is undeniably domestic, as illustrated by the **ANEMONE** lamp, designed by Finnish designers Mari Relander and Anna Katriina Tilli. The lamp is inspired by delicate bobbin-lace tablecloths, and the pattern is adapted from the **VUOKKO** lace series designed by Finnish lace-maker Eeva-Liisa Kortelahti. Fragments of lace (made by Arja Virtanen and Hellevi Wikgren) are attached to a hand-blown glass shade, which is also decorated with a frosted lace motif.

The intricate nature of bobbin lace is used to very different effect by Niels van Eijk in his glass-fibre **BOBBIN LACE LAMP** (2002). This is a lamp without a bulb, hand-knotted from a 500-metre skein of glass fibre optics, so that the shade becomes the light source itself. Lace is also the inspiration for Finnish artist Helena Hietanen, whose work entitled **TECHNOLACE** involves using hand-knotting techniques to create a large-scale fibre-optic art work. The work, which was first shown in Helsinki in 1996 and then at the Venice Biennale in 1997, is reconfigured for each site-specific context and has been exhibited in galleries all over the world. It was originally created as a response to an exhibition theme of handicraft, women and technology.

Lace-making is traditionally a gendered activity, and there is something poignant about the marriage of light with lace-making. Traditionally, lace-makers working at night would produce their intricate work using a candle or rush light surrounded by water-filled glass flasks to intensify the meagre light available.

BOBBIN LACE LAMP
500m glass fibre, light projector
Niels van Eijk, self-production
the Netherlands
2002

DETAIL OF TECHNOLACE LIGHT SCULPTURE
Optical fibre, light projectors
Helena Hietanen, Finland
1997–2003
Courtesy of Galerie Anhava

ANEMONE LAMP
Frosted hand-blown glass, bobbin
lace, halogen bulb
Mari Relander and Anna Katriina
Tilli, self-production, Finland
2002

← →
CAVEMAN LIGHTS
Nomex® paper roll, bulb
Georg Baldele, self-production, UK
2000

Making objects by hand is important as both a theme and a process for many designers, but it is not always an end in itself. Georg Baldele, an Austrian designer based in London, is interested in both industrial materials and the mass-production potential of objects that start life by being made by hand. Baldele uses industrial materials in highly untypical ways, creating visual effects that are brought to life by light. His **CAVEMAN** lights (2000) are conical towers of unfurled tape, made from a material that offers different degrees of transparency as the tape unwinds. The material used for this is Nomex®, which is made by Dupont. This is a fireproof industrial tape used for various applications, including transformer insulation, filters for industrial chimneys and firefighters' clothing. It is a costly and durable material, which has a yellowish colour to it and therefore provides a warm-coloured light. Although initially wanting to find a suitable transparent fabric, Baldele found that the coloured effect of Nomex suggested the light qualities of traditional paper lanterns.

'There is a problem with using specialist materials like this,' he says. 'The lights look like they are made of paper, which everyone expects to be cheap.' Baldele has also tried producing the idea with different markets in mind. He collaborated with Habitat on the paper-hanging lights, and also with the design company Artificial to produce the lights in limited quantities for the British design outlet SCP. His aim is to reach a much wider market with his products, but without losing control of the quality and execution of the final product.

A BEAUTIFUL OBJECT WILL NOT WORK UNLESS IT PROVIDES THE RIGHT QUALITY OF LIGHT FOR ITS INTENDED ENVIRON—MENT
GEORG BALDELE

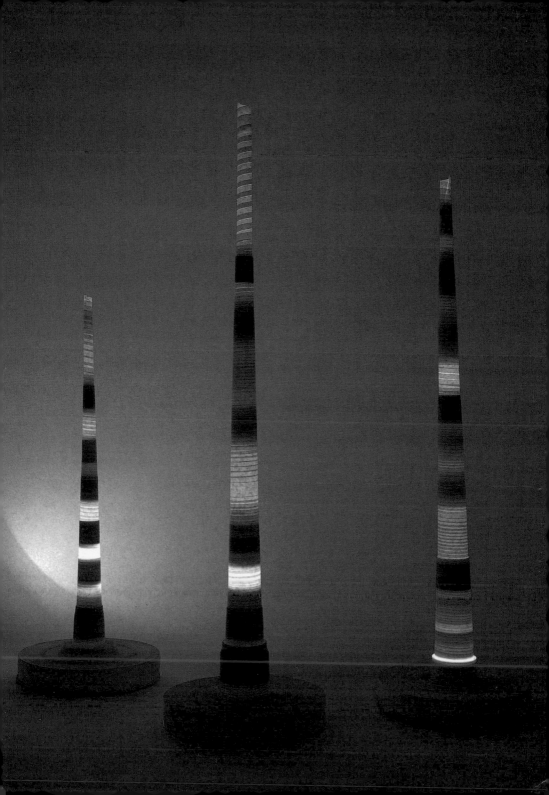

NIAGARA LIGHT
Glass ball fabric strips, fluorescent bulb
Georg Baldele, self-production, UK
1999

Another highly effective application of industrial material can be seen in Baldele's **NIAGARA** light. The **NIAGARA** light is produced from a pliable sheet material made up of glass beads set in resin. The material was developed through an unlikely investigation:

> 'I wanted to do a night light for children, based on an egg-timer, where the light would get dimmer as the sands of the timer slowly ran out. I was looking for a translucent material like sand and found the glass beads which are the waste product from crystal production. This substance is used in various ways – it has reflective properties so it is used in road surfaces and light-reflective paints. I experimented with incorporating the glass beads into fabrics – embedding them into a wire mesh, and fixing them into a resin to make a pliable fabric.'

The result, when hung and lit with neon, is a shimmering curtain of watery light. Baldele first used the material for window displays, and later for various interior installations, including one at the London Design Museum in 2003. Each installation is unique, as Baldele says that 'a beautiful object will not work unless it also provides the right quality of light for its intended environment'.

Industrial glass is also the basis for a light by Italian designer Paolo Ulian. His **FLUXUS** lamp (2002) manufactured by Luminara, incorporates Pyrex glass in its 'raw' industrial form. The glass is sold in 12-millimetre-diameter tubes, and Ulian has set 40 of the tubes into an aluminium base around a lamp. The tubes are heated and bent slightly in the middle, so that they fan outwards. Once set into the base, they can be rotated to create different configurations. 'I wanted to use Pyrex because it is less expensive than other kinds of glass, so that it's possible in one light to use a large quantity of material.'

FLUXUS LAMP
Aluminium, pyrex, halogen bulb
Paolo Ulian, Luminara, Italy
2002

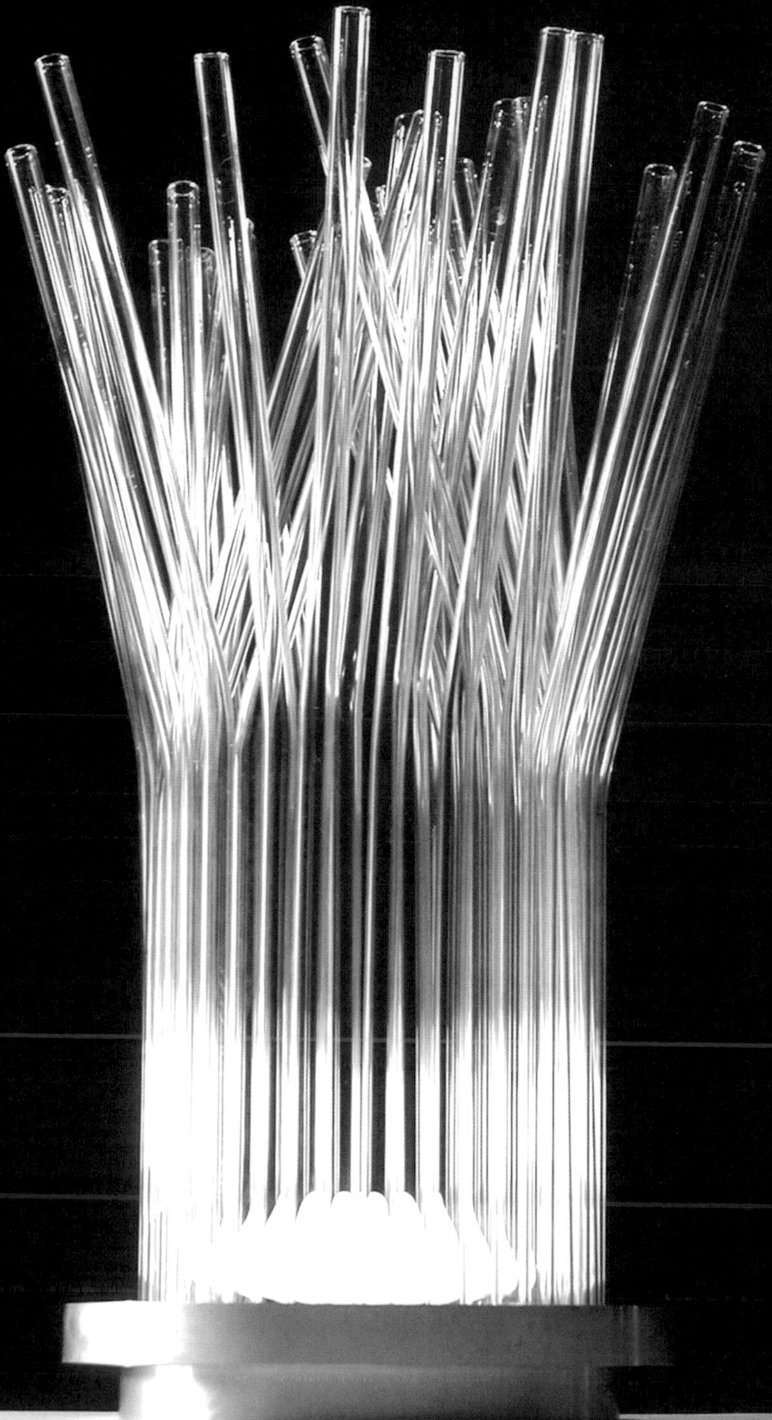

HUUPHUUP LAMPS
Acrylic knitted fibre, epoxy
resin, incandescent bulbs
The Monkey Boys, self-production
2001

The Dutch designer Bertjan Pot has produced an unusual means of creating light shades, which demonstrates how a process of material experimentation can result in both likely and unlikely effects. As a student, Pot experimented with a knitted glass-fibre textile to create product forms. The material, which came as a stretchy knitted tube, was soaked in resin and vacuum formed, leaving a hard and light shell when dry. The fabrication process was not intended specifically for lighting (he also made a side-table), but the resulting seamless and translucent forms were ideal for this use. His **HUUPHUUP** knitted lamps were formed around balloons (the first experiments were with condoms), which were removed once the shells were made. Once the process was established, Pot switched to an acrylic knitted fabric, which was cheaper and easier to use than the glass fibre, and also came in a range of colours and patterns.

Any investigation of this nature can leave a studio full of unused materials, and Pot used some of these 'waste' products to create the **RANDOM** light in 2002. Left with a quantity of glass yarn from an early attempt to knit the glass-fibre fabric himself, he wrapped the resin-soaked yarn around a large balloon to create a slightly different effect. This process is now being used for furniture, with carbon fibre being wrapped around a regular (rather than an inflated) mould.

'I've since found out that in the 1970s people used to make lamps at home using a similar method,' Pot commented, 'only they would use a balloon, ordinary string and wood glue. Long live high tech materials!' The **RANDOM** light is in production with the company Moooi. Another of Pot's prototypes, the **FOLD UP** light, shows that hands-on making and problem solving play a part in his design process. This large, textile light shade with two flexible glass fibres and a reflective lining folds up, and 'pops' open when flexed to form a tent-like shade.

MAKING A SHAPE WITH A BULB IS EASY — YOU MAKE THE SHAPE, PUT IN THE BULB AND IT'S DONE. MAKING A FUNCTIONAL PIECE OF LIGHTING IS SOMETHING ELSE

BERTJAN POT

RANDOM LIGHT
Fibreglass, epoxy resin, incandescent bulb
Bertjan Pot, Moooi, the Netherlands
2002

→
FOLD UP LIGHT
Textile light shade with reflective lining,
flexible glass-fibre tubes, incandescent bulb
Bertjan Pot, self-production,
the Netherlands
2003

AQUA FLOOR LAMP
Woven nylon, monofilament,
steel stand
Sharon Marston, self-production,
UK
2002

Many of the products featured here show the blurring of the boundaries between product design and other disciplines, such as textiles and fashion, as well as fine art. Although not strictly lighting, the incorporation of light technologies into fabrics is a current avenue of exploration that cannot be ignored.

The translation of textile techniques into lighting underpins the approach of British designer Sharon Marston. She studied jewellery design under Caroline Broadhead, a maker known for her interest in conceptual, mixed media work. While a student, Marston became interested in costume as well as in theatre and dance, and produced a series of body-related pieces in her trademark material, woven nylon. She worked for a while in the fashion industry, and then turned to lighting in 1997, when she began producing light shades in woven nylon. She now produces bespoke and batch-production light products as well as installations – including retail window display commissions.

CHANDELIER NO.4
Polypropylene, monofilament,
polymer fibre optics
Sharon Marston for A. J. Browne,
self-production
2002

Marston works with a deliberately limited range of materials – woven nylon, monofilament and polypropylene sheet. Using techniques derived from textiles and costume – folding, pleating, stitching, boning and distressing – she creates complex structures for hanging and standing lights, as well as wall-hangings that incorporate fibre optics. Although some of the designs are batch produced, each is effectively hand-made and therefore unique. She says, 'The material is quite difficult to work with, especially as it is woven on the bias. It slips and moves and is hard to control, so that each light comes out differently.' She is working with manufacturers to develop products for mass production, but also works on bespoke items for individual interior commissions.

At first, Marston's lighting products were simply shades (using off-the shelf lamps and stands), but as she developed her interest in lighting she started to use light as the material itself – weaving with fibre optics, and experimenting with various grades and types of fibre. She has recently started to use glass in her work. She states:

> 'I had no training as a lighting designer, so I came to lighting from a very different perspective, using ideas developed for costume design. There are so many lighting products available off the shelf now, which I can use without great technical knowledge. Fibre optics are relatively easy to handle – they come with a self-contained power supply, and since they do not generate any heat they are safe to work with.'

Marston is interested in the experience, not the physics of lighting, and works in a hands-on manner directly with the material, rather than designing on paper.

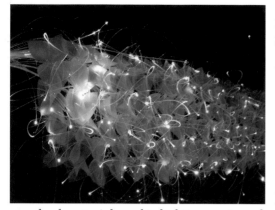

PANEL OF LIGHT
Polypropylene, monofilament,
polymer fibre optics
Sharon Marston, self-production, UK
2002

Polypropylene sheet is a standard material used in lighting, as it can be used with a 'hot' light source without danger. It is an immensely versatile material, but rarely used in an exciting way. Marston cuts the sheet into tiny petal or shell forms; these are stitched together with monofilament and woven with fibre optics. She is also now working with LEDs, which give off much more heat and therefore cannot be combined with certain fabrics. She is currently experimenting with glass as a more durable and heat-resistant material.

Marston's interest in fashion and the body has led to a project in collaboration with the choreographer Yolande Snaith, which is being funded by the British Arts Council. Light has the capacity to be sensual and emotional, so its use in performance can be highly charged. Snaith's work integrates design and the visual arts into dance, using props and objects, and complex and fantastical costumes. Marston first approached Snaith with the idea of working together in the late 1990s, but their collaboration did not really begin until 2003. Marston is creating costumes and set pieces using woven nylon, fibre optics and LEDs (both wearable and static pieces with which the dancers interact). For her, this project is a logical step that brings together her interests in light, materials, the body and movement.

Obviously, lighting is traditionally a central element of scenography, but its use in this sphere by designers without any formal background in theatre work produces some unusual results. Arik Levy has collaborated several times with the Israeli choreographer Ohad Naharin (who is artistic director of the Batsheva Dance Company), for performances in the Netherlands, Finland and Israel. In **KAAMOS** (1997), Levy created the effect of strong light being 'hosed' like a jet of water across the stage and over the faces and bodies of the performers as they crawled over and under the light beams.

PERFORMANCE
Yolande Snaith and Sharon Marston collaboration,
costume and lighting by Sharon Marston
Woven nylon, polypropylene, monofilament,
polymer fibre optics
2002 production, debuts 2004,
touring in UK and internationally

KAAMOS
Lighting design by Arik Levy
(detail)
1997

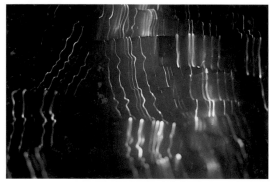

NO FRILLS RUCHED FABRIC LAYERS
Polymer optical fibre, lycra,
nylon monofilament, tungsten
halogen light source.
Sarah Taylor, limited batch
production, made for Jerwood
Applied Arts Prize, UK
2002

Both fibre optics and phosphorescent fabrics are being used to great effect by textile artists and fashion designers. Two British artists, Sophie Roet and Sarah Taylor, have developed applications for using light technologies with fabric. Taylor's work, shortlisted for the Jerwood Prize in 2002, is based on the use of fibre optics woven into fabric works. Roet (who has also worked with leading fashion designers such as Alexander McQueen) uses phosphorescent yarns with a devoré technique to produce light-sensitive, three-dimensional surfaces.

The idea of 'wearable light' is just one aspect of the increasing incorporation of technologies into clothing and body adornment. [23] However, the transformation of 'hardware' (light and power sources, cables, wires and fibres) into 'software' (fabrics) is still in its infancy. Clothing designers working with lighting technologies are hampered by the relative inflexibility of materials and technologies, and the development of flexible light sources and materials is still in its early stages. LEDs can generate as much light as an incandescent bulb, at a fraction of the size and using a fraction of the energy. Fibre optics have the flexibility to be worn on the body, but need a substantial power supply attached to them. But any wearable lighting still needs to be attached to a weighty battery pack in order to work.

BALADEUSE
Ultrasonically welded PVC, polyurethane gel,
compact fluorescent bulb
Izumi Kohama and Xavier Moulin, Ixilab, Japan
2001

The idea of wearable lighting products is therefore still in its infancy. The San Diego-based designer Janet Hansen produces wearable illumination, usually made for artists, clubbers and performers. The garments are lit with LEDs and electroluminescent wire, and sometimes linked to sound sensors. In 2002 Hansen collaborated with Ingo Maurer to produce a collection of unique garments entitled **LIGHT MESSAGES**, which incorporated digital patterns and LED text messages (see p. 16–17). Tokyo-based Ixilab (the partnership of Xavier Moulin and Izumi Kohama) have developed a prototype product called **BALADEUSE** (2001). This is an ultrasonically welded PVC bag filled with a polyurethane gel into which a compact fluorescent bulb is inserted. It is not intended primarily as clothing, but as a soft lighting form that can take on the shape of whatever object or surface it is placed upon. When the product is 'worn', it is draped over a shoulder or around the neck like a scarf. Ken Yokomizo, a Japanese designer based in Milan, has created **WEAIREVER** (2003), a series of light products that can be worn like rucksacks, jackets or hats, and which are battery operated and illuminated with LEDs. They are meant to be worn after dark for safety or for fun, or used as portable lamps at home.

The future development of wearable and personalized light products is dependent upon technological developments in materials and the miniaturization of power sources. Light-emitting materials, such as those developed for the electronics industry for flat and flexible displays, will doubtless find other design applications. One such example is organic light-emitting display (OLED) technology. Currently under development is a method of printing chemical materials on to flat surfaces, which emit coloured light when subjected to an electrical current. Lighted displays could therefore be printed on to packaging, clothing fabrics and wall coverings. Another possibility is nanotechnology – already, fluorescent molecules are being tested as a possible organic light-emitting material for LEDs.

←
WEAIREVER WEARABLE LIGHT
Fabric, fasteners and LEDs
Ken Yokomizo, Italy
2003
Photograph by Lorenso Barassi

—→
LUCIFERAS JACKET
Plastic optical fibre
Grado Zero Espace, Corpo Nove (Karada Italia),
Italy
2002

Electroluminescent sheet and film, a product commonly used for lighted signage, offers other possibilities to both lighting and fashion designers. It is made from a very thin layer of light-emitting phosphor placed between two thin electrodes, one of which is translucent (allowing light to escape). Used by designers such as Karim Rashid and Arik Levy, it is also the subject of clothing experimentation by Pia Myrvold of US-based fashion house Cybercouture. Myrvold's innovative on-going work with light in clothing includes the use of light-reflective piping on garments (Spring/Summer 2003 collection) and fabrics made through bonding reflective PVC panels (Reflexology collection, 2004). Future work will include clothing that incorporates LED panels, so that light effects can be controlled by the wearer.

The experimental Italian textiles company Karada Italia, owner of the Corpo Nove brand, has also been developing ways of incorporating light into clothing. Its research division, Grado Zero Espace, is focused on textile and garment innovation, and on bringing ideas from the aerospace, medical and construction industries into garment technology. Its **LUCIFERAS** jacket (2002) used plastic optical fibre (as opposed to the more usual glass optical fibre) woven into fabric to produce a flexible material. The plastic optical fibre is made of an acrylic core with a thin cladding of fluorinated polymer, and is more durable, flexible and less costly than glass optical fibre. Fabric made of woven fibre optics, however, has limited uses for clothing, as it does not give enough flexibility and comfort to either the fabric or the wearer, and also requires a garment to be fitted with a battery pack. The company is now developing light-emitting fabrics using OLED technology. Fabric is coated with a liquid polymer solution that can be illuminated universally when an electric current is passed through it. As fashion keeps pace with developments in the electronics industry (such as flexible display technology), the idea of wearable light and information-laden clothing becomes more possible.

'We can turn on a lamp with a caress, we can take our temperature by placing a very thin strip of plastic on our forehead, or we can wear an outfit that changes colour according to our body temperature.' [24]

In his influential book 'The Material of Invention' (1986), Ezio Manzini proposed that future materials would be characterized by lightness, flexibility, mutability, reactivity and intelligence. He also indicated the growing importance of surface in objects – there would be surfaces with memory, with the ability to transmit information, with a responsiveness to heat, light and touch. In all these developments, light plays a crucial role as both medium and message. Information can be beamed as light across fibre-optic cables, and LED technology will help in the replacement of the cathode ray tube with flat-screen displays.

These future materials and technologies are now part of our everyday experience, providing an infrastructure for today's information society. Designers continue to explore their poetic possibilities in objects that display the properties predicted by Manzini. We have objects that can 'feel', materials that 'remember' and reactive, information-laden surfaces that are little more than membranes. Rather than dehumanizing the material world, such developments can be harnessed to produce objects that we can connect with on a more personal and emotional level.

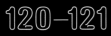

120–121

SILVER STRIPED DRESS
Electro-luminscent fabric
Reflexology collection
Spring/Summer 2004,
Pia Myrvold, Cybercouture,
USA
2002

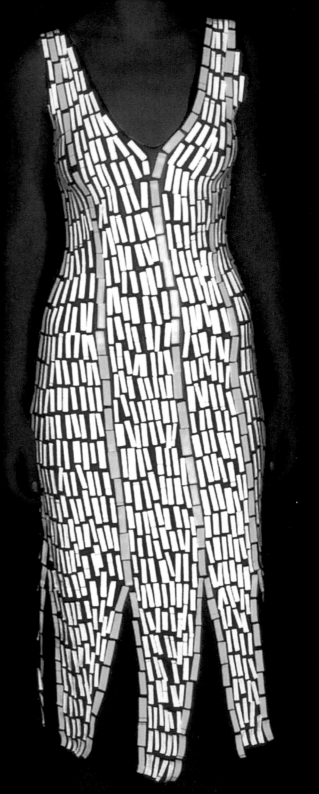

WE CAN
TURN ON A
LAMP WITH
A CARESS,
WE CAN
TAKE OUR
TEMPERATURE
BY PLACING
A VERY THIN
STRIP OF
PLASTIC
ON OUR
FOREHEAD,
OR WE CAN
WEAR AN
OUTFIT THAT
CHANGES
COLOUR
ACCORDING
TO OUR
BODY
TEMPERATURE

EZIO MANZINI

SOCIAL and **ANTI-SOCIAL LIGHTS**
Resin, electronics
Michael Anastassiadies, UK
2001
Courtesy of Walker Arts
Center, USA
Photograph by
Cameron Wittig

BUBBLE LIGHT
Silicon, LEDs and rechargeable batteries
Aaron Rincover, Mathmos, UK
2000

Lighting will become more responsive to immediate environmental conditions such as heat, sound and touch, like Aaron Rincover's silicon **BUBBLE** light (2000), which responds to a squeeze of the hand. Michael Anastassiades has developed a lighting concept that reacts to its social environment. The **SOCIAL** and **ANTI-SOCIAL LIGHTS** (2001) are noise-activated – the **SOCIAL** light comes on when it 'hears' conversation, encouraging and enhancing social interaction. The **ANTI-SOCIAL** light gradually dims when it hears noise, but comes alive to silence, in order to provide light for quiet contemplative activities such as reading. In the future, light might not come at the flick of a switch – you may be able to just talk nicely to your lamps, and they will switch themselves on for you.

> 'Between us two it's not a star at all.
> It's a new patented electric light.'
>
> **ROBERT FROST,**
> **'THE LITERATE FARMER AND THE PLANET VENUS', 1942.**

FURTHER RESEARCH

A substantial annual review of contemporary lighting can be found in the International Design Yearbook (published annually, Thames & Hudson, London). Considerable information on contemporary lighting design is included in design and style magazines such as Abitare, Blueprint, Domus, Elle Decoration, Frame, I.D. – International Design, Intermuros, Metropolis and Wallpaper*. There is also a specialist press for the lighting industry, which includes publications such as the journal International Lighting Review (published by Philips, Eindhoven). The National Art Library at the V&A Museum has a substantial collection of trade literature relating to lamps and lighting.

Bauer, Helmut (ed), Ingo Maurer: Making Light, Nazraeli Press, Tuscon, Arizona 1992.

Bowers, Brian, Lengthening the Day, A History of Lighting Technology, Oxford University Press, Oxford 1998.

Braddock, Sarah E. and O'Mahony, Marie, Techno Textiles, Revolutionary Fabrics for Fashion and Design, Thames & Hudson, London 1998.

Byars, Mel, 50 Lights, Innovations in Design and Materials, Rotovision, New York 1997.

Clegg, Brian, Light Years, An Exploration of Mankind's Enduring Fascination with Light, Piatkus, London 2001.

Crowley, John E., The Invention of Comfort, Sensibilities & Design in Early Modern Britain & Early America, The John Hopkins University Press, Baltimore & London 2000.

Dillon, Maureen, Artificial Sunshine: A Social History of Domestic Lighting, National Trust, London 2002.

Fiell, Charlotte and Peter (eds), Designing the 21st Century, Taschen, Cologne 2001.

Hinte, Ed van, Eternally Yours: Visions of Product Endurance, 010 Publishers, Rotterdam 1997.

Höger, Hans, The Tizio Light by Richard Sapper, Verlag Form, Frankfurt am Main 1997.

Lupton, Ellen, Skin, Surface, Substance and Design, Cooper-Hewitt National Design Museum (Smithsonian Institution), Laurence King Publishing Ltd, London 2002.

Manzini, Ezio, The Material of Invention: Materials and Design, The Design Council, London 1989.

Myerson, Jeremy and Katz, Sylvia, Lamps & Lighting, Conran Octopus, London 1990.

Myerson, Jeremy, International Lighting Design, Laurence King Publishing Ltd, London 1996.

Porcelli, V. Lorenzo, International Lighting Design, Rockport Publishers, Rockport, Mass. 1991.

Ramakers, Renny, Droog Design: Spirit of the Nineties, 010 Publishers, Rotterdam 1998.

Rashid, Karim, I Want to Change the World, Thames & Hudson, London 2001.

Schivelbusch, Wolfgang, Disenchanted Night: The Industrialization of Light in the Nineteenth Century (trans. A. Davies), The University of California Press, California 1988.

Stichting Interieur (exhibition catalogue), Licht= Light + Design, 16th Biennial for Interior Design Creativity, Kortrijk, Belgium 1998.

Sudjic, Deyan, The Lighting Book, Mitchell Beazley, London 1993.

Tanizaki, Jun'ichirō, In Praise of Shadows, Cape, London 1991.

Turner, Janet, Lighting, An Introduction to Light, Lighting and Light Use, B.T. Batsford Ltd, London 1994.

Wanders, Marcel & Joris, Yvonne G.J.M. (eds), Wanders Wonders: Design for a New Age, 010 Publishers, Rotterdam 1999.

Zijl, Ida van and Boyer, Maurice, Droog Design 1991–1996, Centraal Museum, Utrecht 1997.

NOTES

All quotations in the text, unless otherwise stated, are based on interviews with the author.

1. Ezio Manzini, The Material of Invention: Materials and Design, The Design Council, London 1989, p. 159.

2. Ezio Manzini, p. 203.

3. Ingo Maurer, Catalogue 2000/2001, p. 28.

4. Kazuhiro Yamanaka, personal statement, 2002.

5. According to the Sustainability Committee of the International Association of Lighting Designers.

6. www.eternally-yours.org Ed van Hinte, Eternally Yours: Visions of Product Endurance, 010 Publishers, Rotterdam 1997.

7. Jun'ichirō Tanizaki, In Praise of Shadows, Cape, London 1991, p. 57.

8. Jun'ichirō Tanizaki, p. 45.

9. Wolfgang Schivelbusch, Disenchanted Night: The Industrialization of Light in the Nineteenth Century (trans. A. Davies), The University of California Press, 1988, p. 181.

10. John E. Crowley, The Invention of Comfort, Sensibilities & Design in Early Modern Britain & Early America, The John Hopkins University Press, Baltimore & London 2000, p. 136.

11. Brian Bowers, Lengthening the Day, A History of Lighting Technology, Oxford University Press, Oxford 1998, p. 162.

12. A.H. Barr, Foreword to Machine Art, Museum of Modern Art, Harry N. Abrams Inc., 1934, reprinted 1991, unpaginated.

13. Personal recollection from A.C. Ratcliffe, quoted in Brian Bowers, Lengthening the Day: A History of Lighting Technology, Oxford University Press, 1998, p. 169.

14. Jonathan M. Woodham, 'Managing British Design Reform II: The Film Deadly Lampshade – An Ill-fated Episode in the Politics of "Good Taste"', Journal of Design History, Issue 2, 1996, pp. 101–115.

15. Paola Antonelli, in Mel Byars, 50 Lights, Innovations in Design and Materials, Rotovision, New York, 1997.

16. Arik Levy, quoted in Mel Byars, On/Off – New Electronic Products. Laurence King Publishers, London 2001, p. 45.

17. Marcel Wanders, Wanders Wonders: Designs for a New Age, 010 Publishers, Rotterdam, 1999, p. 24.

18. Quoted in Renny Ramakers, Droog Design: Spirit of the Nineties, 010 Publishers, Rotterdam 1998, p. 103.

19. Maurer, quoted at www.moma.org.

20. Marcel Duchamp, Ingénieur de temps perdu, Belfond, Paris 1967, pp. 84–5 quoted in Emmanuel Guigon, El Objeto Surrealista, IVAM Centre Julio Gonzalez, Valencia 1997 (English translation), p. 274.

21. Benjamin, Count Rumford, The Complete Works, Boston, undated, Vol. 4, p. 106. Quoted in Wolfgang Schivelbusch, p. 167.

22. Jane Pavitt, 'Designing in the Digital Age', Architectural Design, Vol. 69, 11–12, 1999, Profile 142, pp. 96–9.

23. For an exploration of this theme, see Andrew Bolton, The SuperModern Wardrobe, V&A Publications, London 2002.

24. Ezio Manzini, The Material of Invention: Materials and Design, The Design Council, London 1989, p. 26.

INDEX